Andre Perry

Some of Us Are Very Hungry Now

Essays

To Hyun's mom
– Please enjoy
this book!
Thank you
for reading!

Two Dollar Radio
Books too loud to ignore

Two Dollar Radio
Books too loud to Ignore

WHO WE ARE Two Dollar Radio is a family-run outfit dedicated to reaffirming the cultural and artistic spirit of the publishing industry. We aim to do this by presenting bold works of literary merit, each book, individually and collectively, providing a sonic progression that we believe to be too loud to ignore.

TwoDollarRadio.com

Proudly based in
Columbus
OHIO

@TwoDollarRadio

@TwoDollarRadio

/TwoDollarRadio

Love the
PLANET?
So do we.

Printed on Rolland Enviro.
This paper contains 100% post-consumer fiber, is manufactured using renewable energy - Biogas and processed chlorine free.

100%   PCF   BIO GAS   PERMANENT

Printed in Canada

SOME RECOMMENDED LOCATIONS FOR READING *SOME OF US ARE VERY HUNGRY NOW*: In the club (before the show), in a small bedroom with an 8-track player, or pretty much anywhere because books are portable and the perfect technology!

AUTHOR PHOTO→ Zak Neumann

COVER PHOTO→ Abe Bingham, *Chavez Sunset*, 2011

WE MUST ALSO POINT OUT THAT: The stories in this book reflect the author's recollection of events. Some names, locations, and identifying characteristics have been changed to protect the privacy of those depicted. Dialogue has been re-created from memory.

CONTENTS

Coastland

Heartland

Heart

Well
Here it comes
Here comes the sound
The sound of confusion

J. Spaceman & Sonic Boom, "Walkin' with Jesus"

Some of Us Are Very Hungry Now

Coastland

Language and Other Weapons

The screen is black. The sounds of bodies rustling in leaves can be heard. They are the sounds of love.

NARRATOR (VOICE OVER)
Being black is like having a chronic disease because someone can always call you a nigger and you know they eventually will. You just don't know when it's going to come at you or how it's going to come. Will you get called a nigger out loud or in a more deceptive if equally devastating way? Life goes on for some time without incident and then the affliction bites you again, reminds you that it's still there. These "nigger moments"—the points in time when black people are forced to recall their blackness in a way that brings shame to their existence—engender self-hate over time. The hate can twist the strongest heart, reducing one's composure to a vicious growl. The black lashes out at his environment but his hateful words and angry jabs will only quicken his failure.

DISSOLVE TO:

EXT. FIELD—EVENING

WIDE SHOT: Black-and-white film. Nestled within the tall grass of a field, a YOUNG BLACK MAN and a YOUNG BLACK WOMAN make love on the ground. The camera slowly zooms in on the couple. A dress is pulled up around her waist. Their faces are filled with excitement.

NARRATOR (VOICE OVER—CONT'D)
Consider a character from Toni Morrison's
The Bluest Eye, Cholly Breedlove. Morrison
first published the novel in the United States
in 1970, but it takes place in the years before
and after the Great Depression. On the night
Cholly loses his virginity to a beautiful country
girl, Darlene, he is subjected to the humiliation
of a nigger moment.

As CHOLLY and DARLENE continue to make love, the crunching of footsteps on twigs and stalks of grass can be heard. A light shines across CHOLLY's back. The girl freezes. CHOLLY senses her change in emotion and turns around. His eyes meet with the faces of two WHITE MEN. WHITE MAN 1 holds a lantern. Both men are smiling.

WHITE MAN 1
Get on wid it. An' make it good, nigger. Make
it good.

CHOLLY's lover turns cold. He continues the act but it is no longer love. The WHITE MEN stand there, chuckling for a minute or so and then they walk away. Their voices grow more distant until all that can be heard are the sounds of the country night.

NARRATOR (VOICE OVER)

This incident leaves Cholly scarred for life. It is a watershed moment of shame upon which others will build. Eventually, self-hate will implode the young black man. He will embrace alcoholism and begin to despise his wife and his children. Ultimately, he will rape his young daughter. It would take the space of another novel to fully understand how the incident had scarred DARLENE.

CUT TO:

A close up on CHOLLY's face. His face, a scowl. CHOLLY raises himself up from DARLENE. She is silent, frozen with pain. His hands loom menacingly as though he might strangle her.

CUT TO:

BLACK

The sounds of CHILDREN PLAYING can be heard.

DISSOLVE TO:

EXT. FIELD—DAY

Color film. A group of fourth grade boys are playing a game of football on a black top. These are St. Albans boys, students at one of Washington, D.C.'s most prestigious private schools. They wear blazers, ties, turtlenecks, and slacks. They play their game in the shadow of the National Cathedral. A tall kid steps up to the line of scrimmage with the football in his hands. His team of five receivers joins him.

That's ME, age 10, scrawny and lanky, at the right end of the line, getting excited to run a pass route. The QB hikes the ball and the PASS RUSHER stands in front of him, READY TO STRIKE.

PASS RUSHER
One-Mississippi. Two-Mississippi.

BURNING my defender down the field I wave my hand to let the QB know I am open. Our eyes connect and he sends the ball into the air. As it comes closer to my hands something blurs. My coordination escapes me and the ball DROPS to the ground.

A TEAMMATE walks by me, angry at the missed opportunity. He HITS me on the shoulder and looks me in the eye.

TEAMMATE
Faggot.

ME
Fuck you.

Recollect these:

1. A year-long beating in fourth grade
   a. Faggot, a nickname
   b. Mouth, a weapon
   c. Nigger, an insinuation

2. A failure to fit a part
   a. Catch footballs
   b. Play Nintendo
   c. Shhh yer little mouth, teacher don't wanna
      hear about yer fag-tag

3. A face crushed into pillows, upstairs
   a. At home the
   b. Parents hope that
   c. Moments will pass

4. A list of boys' school rules
   a. Class shuffled out like cards
   b. You don't pick your hand, you just play it
      the best you can
   c. Get stuck or be ready to stick

5. A fifth and sixth grader
   a. Stand up straight
   b. Look through them sharply
   c. Laugh down at them and look up now:
      son, you're popular

The well-dressed, would-be men of St. Albans pass through the halls on their way to class, toting L.L.Bean and JanSport backpacks filled to the brim with selections from the literary canon. I walk down the hallway, book bag weighing me down. I wear awkward glasses and an oxford, one neck-size too big. My red tie is done up in a rough, bulky knot and my khakis hang slightly below my waist. A blazer without buttons. I am a freshman now and any prestige I amassed in grade school has been erased. The slate is fresh and naked.

In James Weldon Johnson's 1912 *The Autobiography of an Ex-Colored Man*, the central character, a bi-racial man who is light enough to pass for white, finds that he still can't escape nigger moments even when he isn't the primary victim. As he moves through the early 20th century South considering whether or not to live as black or white, he witnesses the lynching and burning of a black man. This traumatic moment drives the character to embrace a white existence for the rest of his life, forever leaving behind the black elements of his heritage. He fails to realize that he will always be sensitive to black issues: He will always be the invisible victim of nigger moments. Someone in the room shouts "nigger" and laughs. He smiles along, cringes beneath the false pretense of his light skin. Even in passing he cannot transcend the pain.

There is a new weapon in high school: Anything a black kid does that breaks from the stereotype of what it "means" to be black is dubbed as "manipulated." How do you know if you're manipulated? Do you listen to Guns N' Roses or like the Boss? Do you wear tight, torn Levi's jeans instead of baggy Hilfigers? Do you get good grades and get them with pride? Do you talk with an accent fitting for white, college-bound gentlemen? Have you ever dreamed of kissing a white girl? If you answered yes to any of these questions then you might be manipulated.

As the older, cool kids run the manipulation trials, they substitute questions of blackness into the subtext of *The Crucible*. Like Africans selling slaves to white men on their shores, the prosecutors are often black, but even some of the popular white students aren't afraid to move in for the kill either. And like being called a faggot in fourth grade, you don't go to the dean about being called manipulated. That action would in fact be considered manipulated—even the dean might call you out on that one.

Roosevelt is in tenth grade. He is physically imposing, a star lineman on the varsity football team. He is also black, often pissed off, and he will personally lead the inquisition of my psyche during freshman year of high school. I have known his family for years. I am friends with his younger brother and our parents get along. But the family history brings little pause to Roosevelt's crusade against what he sees as my white cultural leanings.

I stand outside of the high school's main entrance, leaning against the frame of the large wooden dais, observing the expanse of the campus, the National Cathedral posing in the background. It is a free-dress day. Most kids have left their preppy uniforms at home. Some boys, anticipating their business-casual wardrobe of the future, wear golf shirts tucked into jeans. Others are simply wearing jeans and t-shirts. I've got my jeans on, torn like the denim of Kurt Cobain. Roosevelt walks by me. Looks me up and down, and, seeing my alternative rock outfit, produces a frown and a comment: "Why are you such a sellout?"

Dearest Saint Alban,

The quandary you've put me in is most disturb-ing. The layers of contradiction are disori-enting. Who put these "non-black" clothes — the blazers, turtlenecks and ties — on my back in the first place? Didn't you ask me to be one of tomorrow's champions? Haven't you constructed me in your divine image of the beautiful, strong and rich Caucasian man? Then why do you spite me when I play the role so well?

Your friend,

Andre

Walking into a bathroom, I see two white sophomores sitting up on the windowsill, talking about rap music. We are not friends but I choose to intervene and correct them on the finer points of hip-hop. One of them demands of me, "Well what do you know… You're not a real nigger."

Get on wid it. An' make it good.

On a warm spring day, with flowers blooming, the tide of the seasons changing, sweaters and jackets retiring, and semesters growing shorter, I feel angry. I am hanging out in the student lounge where we fill ourselves with Coca-Cola and microwave pizzas. Dennis, a fellow freshman, white and accruing more upperclassmen abuse than myself, is getting pushed around by another group of kids. At age 15 his whole style is tall, goofy, and uncomfortable. He gets knocked down to the ground by a bigger kid—*punk*—and the older students laugh. He just curls up and hides his face. I've been there and felt it before and I'm embarrassed to be capable of empathizing with such a pathetic existence. There's a lull in the beating so I stand up and kick him in the back while he's lying on the ground. I kick him to get a few laughs. I kick him to feel better. And I get those laughs, but at the cost that he will never forget. At the cost that I can never take it back. I only feel better for a few fleeting seconds.

All grown up, Dennis is an upstanding citizen engineering political campaigns—believing the American republic can work. We periodically cross paths at reunions and gatherings of the old D.C. scene. He's not goofy anymore, but rather he's endearing and cheerful. We share beers and laughs but I can see him looking behind my eyes. He knows that I know that he has not forgotten: You kicked me in the back, motherfucker.

* * *

Cutting down Interstate 5. The drive is long and the air conditioning's been broken for years. We sweat it out in the car as we head farther south on our six-hour trek from San Francisco to Los Angeles. I am post-St. Albans, post-college, post-everything that the East Coast offered me. I have moved to California because its enduring promise of finding a new life resonated with me as I rolled up my diploma and packed my boxes. San Francisco is my new home but the allure of the road, of traveling to other California towns for music, art, and the unknown has become a core practice.

We cruise through the depths of the Central Valley, a gloomy stretch between the Bay Area and So Cal where a dense fog sometimes fills the air and the vast fields of agriculture surround us. The cassette player is permanently jammed and the radio just spits out static, so mostly we talk to each other the whole way down. I am laughing at something one of my friends said, but I am also slightly discomforted when he drops the f-bomb. He is one of the most progressive people I know and a deeply intelligent individual, so it contradicts everything I have ever heard him say in defense of equity for all people. "Hey man, do you have a problem with gay people?" I ask. "You're always calling out people as 'fags.'"

He turns to me and in earnest says, "No, not at all. *Not at all.* I am totally fine with gay people. I just hate faggots."

I'm not quite laughing. I'm not quite angry. I am entirely unsettled. I am reminded at how many times I have also participated in the muddled, callous vortex of humor and disrespect.

A double-edged vocabulary list—*nigger* and *faggot*—sowing unity or drawing blood depending which side of the blade is used and, of course, who happens to be using it. Gay people call each other fags and we call each other niggers when none of us is required to do so. A gay person might say to another with a smile, *oh don't be such a fag*, and a black friend will call out to me, *what's up, my nigga*, and it will feel warm. Alternately, a gay person might look at another with a scowl and scream, *get out of the room, you dirty faggot*, just as a black person might grimace at me from the window of a car, their hand in the shape of a gun, and yell, *step off my block, nigger*. Human language bends so flexibly; such subtle shifts in situation and intonation turn salutations into weapons. And to cross the line, to take our malleable words outside of our own circles: for any non-black person to call me a nigger or for me to call anyone a faggot twists those volatile weapons into sharp tools of torture. There was a time when I would have called a friend of mine a fag for being too picky, too annoying or soft. I was stabbing wildly into the air, my blade ripping spiritual flesh—I was too foolish, too uncaring to see the damage.

In his 2008 HBO comedy special, *Kill the Messenger*, Chris Rock opines at considerable length about appropriate uses of the word *faggot*, although one must wonder who granted him—straight black man—license to stand as authority on the topic. "If you're having a fight with somebody," he says, "you should be able to say whatever you think is going to hurt this person the most... you one-legged bastard."

He discusses actor Isaiah Washington's dismissal from the television show *Grey's Anatomy*. Washington had allegedly called fellow cast-member T.R. Knight a faggot during an argument. Rock questions, "What if the person [Washington] called a faggot was acting like a faggot?" Washington is black and Knight would later come out as gay. While there is no end to the amount of white people who need to be corrected on their use of homophobic language, there is also a sickness within black culture—American and elsewhere—that rallies against the rights and emotions of gay people. I have observed it my entire life—through friends, family, the music I listen to, and the popular figures I follow. At my worst moments I have been a participant in it. Our culture vigorously reminds us that no one really wants to be on the bottom alone; that when given the opportunity to strike out with language, legislation, or other forms of violence against others—despite our own battles for fairness—we might indulge ourselves more than we like to admit. It is not unlike kicking someone in the back when both of you are down.

In his discussion of hate language, Chris Rock clarifies for his audience: "You don't have to be gay to act like a faggot." He explains that if he were sitting at an intersection, singing along to Gwen Stefani's "Hollaback Girl" with such enthusiasm that it caused him to miss the green light, then the driver behind him would have license to call him a faggot. At the punchline, the video cuts to a black man in the audience standing up and clapping. I want to understand why they picked *that* hard cut at *that* moment to the black man standing up and clapping; when someone stands up and claps at a comedian's joke, it's not just an affirmation of humor but a vote of confidence in the ideology that has just been publicly offered. Rock concludes, "Shit, even Elton John would call me a faggot."

Get on wid it. An' make it good.

Castro Street is alive and this is my home. Rainbow flags hang from telephone poles, replacing the day-glo colorama of '60s San Francisco. There are gay men, so many different kinds: the burly leather-adorned bears, the club-kid fashionistas, the Brooks Brothers-clad professionals, the extravagant losers with opiate-streaked eyes, and the elder statesmen wearing their blue denim shirts tucked into blue denim jeans—each strand of their white hair is a stripe of survival from the late 20th century AIDS detonation. Standing here on the streets of gay pride, the Castro is some kind of paradise.

Halloween feels like a gay Christmas in San Francisco: The streets of the Castro fill with thousands of costumed enthusiasts. And how fitting that the city gives this holiday to gay culture. It's the one day when everyone can pretend to be someone else: *Oh darling, you'd make such a good little queenie; it's too bad you're only playing.* Put the costume back in the closet by tomorrow morning.

Is the Castro akin to a gay man's version of early 20th century black Harlem, a safe-haven nestled in a city with more conservative values than its façade would like to admit? This radical openness wouldn't fly elsewhere. So if you're a gay man, you have to make a choice that no one should have to make: Stay here, locked up in the Castro, with all of your people, or venture outside where you'll be subjected to hatred. Maybe on a warm white night they'll come down here to knock a riot upside your head just to remind you that you're a fag in their eyes.

Nella Larsen's Harlem Renaissance-era novel, *Quicksand*, follows a feminine protagonist, a tragic mulatto, who finds herself torn between living within the elitist confines of black Harlem, or living in a white European society that embraces her but still sees her as "the other." Is the Castro so different for young gay kids showing up, green from college on the East Coast, filled with hopes of freedom of expression? They can choose to navigate the "free" but class-structured world of the Castro or swim through the "liberal" seas of San Francisco's other scenes where they are met by smiles, handshakes, and pats on the back, but left to wonder who murmurs "faggot" when they leave the room. At once San Francisco is the most liberal American town and the town where liberals think of themselves as most immune from the -isms they publicly rally against.

It's 2003 and I am 25, black, and frequently straight, and I like living here in the Castro. I walk outside and feel good. I am in the company of the persecuted, people who can empathize with my existential pain; people who know what it's like to be pissed on for years. On top of the empathy, they might even want to fuck me and it feels good to be wanted. Some of my roommates can't stand the long stares but I feed into it. I go to the Pilsner Inn, next to our apartment, behind their backs. I sit alone at the bar and drink glasses of Wild Turkey. They can't always tell if I'm straight or gay in there and I like that I am capable of passing. But even when they know I am straight they don't care because they think, he's black and he's been through enough. I smile, throw back the whiskey, and head out the door to get into trouble on the north side of town.

Dearest Gay Diary:

I can call you a faggot and I know I'm going to get a laugh from somebody. I'm taking something away from you when I do that. I'm making a point. I guess you could call me a nigger and you'd also be making a point. You know, all we're doing here is marking each other as different, something less than the full-blown, all-powerful white male image. We're chipping away at each other's pure sexuality. Niggers can't defend their women and faggots ain't ever gonna be real men. You and I, Gay Diary, we should join forces. We should take ourselves out of the system that plays us against each other.

Yes, I know I should stop using these words but it's so hard because I want to call that guy who cut me off a faggot, and that guy whining in class about the ten-page term paper the teacher assigned, the people in the office who complain when finances are tight and they stop giving us free booze on Fridays and worst of all those politicians whose actions defy the values they preach. They're all fags.

And another thing, Gay Diary, could you give me some room here? And by *give me some room I mean take your hands off my leg, you dirty little fag...* hehe, I called you a fag. Oh dear me, there I go again, Gay Diary. You deserve to be mad at me. I know my hypocrisy comes on hard, like a late-summer rain... hehe, I said hard. I bet you're thinking about a hard dick. In your mouth. I can't quit you, Gay Diary. I try not to hate but with all these people coming down on my skin, sometimes not even knowing it — breaking out the joke that buries the night — I need my hate words too.

Your constant other and forever your brother,

Andre

From: louanne-rachel <louanne-rachel@ gaydiary.com>
Reply-To: "Louanne-Rachel" <louanne-rachel@ gaydiary.com>
Sent: Sunday, June 1, 2002 4:52 PM
To: "Andre Perry" <princehal@hotmail.com>
Subject: RE: Dearest Gay Diary

well andre, you never cease to disgust me but while i've got you here I might as well weigh in. you just remember: every topper needs a bot-tom and my little darkie friend you'll forever

be playing both roles. the cocktail party is
the battlefield and language is the weapon. so
use your firearm of choice. bullets fly in both
directions. en guarde. draw. touché.

you are an eternal thorn in my ass mr. perry.
feel my prick, you cocksucker,

--louanne

i couldn't have given you a straighter answer.

INT. A SOUNDSTAGE IN CHICAGO—DAY
CUE: APPLAUSE

The lights come up and O is sitting in her plush leather chair.
There is an empty seat across from her. She SMILES and
WAVES at the audience.

> **O**
> Welcome back to today's show, everyone. This
> is going to be a tough one, I think. For the first
> time ever I am going to talk about a book that
> is not on my book club list. It is Andre Perry's
> *Faggots Are the New Niggers*.

GASPS in the audience.

> **O** (CONT'D)
> This book is highly controversial right now.
> Mr. Perry is catching heat from all sides for his
> hypocritical views on racism and homophobia.
> Everyone, please welcome Mr. Perry.

ANDRE walks onstage to a mix of applause and disapproving grunts. He SITS down in a leather chair across from O.

> **O**
> Hello, Andre.

> **ANDRE**
> Hey, O.

O places her hand on ANDRE'S knee briefly.

> **O**
> So, Andre, this here is one interesting book. It's short but it sure does shock.

O LOOKS at the audience.
BEAT.

> **O** (CONT'D)
> Tell me, Andre, where does it all come from?

> **ANDRE**
> Well I guess it grew out of an essay that I wrote called "Language and Other Weapons." I published that on my website, naggotsgo-figger.com, and I received quite a reaction so I thought I might squeeze a book out of it and make some money to help with my car payments.

> **O**
> Ha! Ain't that the truth?

Some audience laughter.

O (CONT'D)

But really, what is it inside of you that spawned these radical ideas?

ANDRE

I think it was my own personal issues and, you know, thoughts on the subject matter. I've got this idea that just dealing with being a black man might cause us to lash out, especially with anti-gay language. White men are already using this language so they're not going to stop us from using it. They have no problem with us black folk getting away with homophobia especially within the black community. It spreads us apart even further. Yes, there are a lot of people still throwing around the n-word but seriously let's all admit it's a lot easier to get away with calling someone a faggot or even easier to call their style gay. If Peter Jennings called someone's behavior niggerish on the nightly news he would be cast out but I bet he could get away with calling something gay. He wouldn't get fired—he would just have to make some formal apology and social media would go nuts but eventually we'd see him back on television.

O

Peter Jennings is dead, Andre.

ANDRE

Whatever, he was a fag anyway.

Audience members GASP and BOO. Jump cut to: one MAN in the back row and his RAUCOUS LAUGHTER.

                    O
Moving on. Do you really think people can get
away with anti-gay language?

                  ANDRE
Do you go outside? Do you remember when
Kanye West came out and said: We need to
stop being anti-gay in the hip-hop community.
No one gave a damn. His statement received
minimal coverage from the mainstream or hip-
hop media outlets—and that was way before
he went off the deep end.

O looks distressed.

              ANDRE (CONT'D)
The system, I think, wants black people to use
this language. We're encouraged to because
when we ask for our own rights they can point
their fingers and say you guys call people faggots. And they're right. Anything that makes
us look worse and maintains the divide among
those who should work together keeps the discussion of the real problems further off the
table.

                    O
And where do you stand?

                  ANDRE
I used this language. It was built into my
DNA of growing up in America. I know it's
not right. But the addict is always the addict
even when they're clean. Relapse is always an

available option. And when you try to get better, there's another drug—you don't say faggot, but then you substitute words like *pussy, cunt,* or *bitch*—they all get back to the same idea which is attacking people, attacking sexuality, attacking gender.

O nervously LOOKS at her cue cards.

O

So what I'm hearing from you is that *faggot* really is the new *nigger?*

ANDRE

Well yes and no. The word *nigger* or a "nigger moment" takes away black manhood while *faggot* takes away male sexuality. It's a fine distinction. The erosion of black manhood is the erosion of the patriarchal role of black men. We are made unable to protect our women, and consequently, our children. A black man caught in a nigger moment is no king. When I call your boyfriend a faggot, O, I am saying he is unable to complete the male sexual role in bed. He can only love men and, in a sense, he is left infertile, unable to further his bloodline through traditional sexual means. Gay sex is a dead end in the construct of white male supremacy.

O

So, Andre, why can't we as a people, and why can't you as an upright citizen, bring yourself to stop saying faggot when you know it's wrong?

ANDRE

It's the nigger in me.

O

Cut the tape.

ANDRE

That was a joke!

RAUCOUS MAN IN AUDIENCE

Get on wid it. An' make it good, nigger!

O

Cut the goddamn tape.

Author's Note:

The term "nigger moment" was originally conceived by Aaron McGruder in the *Boondocks* comic strip and television show, although I define it quite differently. Or maybe they're two sides of the same coin.

We Thought We Were Rock 'n' Roll

He was sucking me off and god he looked so hungry. His shoulders were broad, popping out of the straps of his dress. His face was like concrete and his mouth was warm. I'd grab the sides of his face and the stubble would scratch my palms. I turned him around but I couldn't get the condom on. I kept going soft. That's when people stopped watching. It was clear the show was over, their fantasies deflated by my limpness. I kissed him on the cheek and put my pants back on.

Upstairs, out of the dungeon of the sex club, my head was full of coke and whiskey and light beer. The night had started differently. It hadn't been dirty, although beneath the surface, I suppose I have always been dirty, waiting for or even courting something like that, wanting it to happen. Or maybe I had really gone there for a woman and settled for anything with a hole. At any rate, it wasn't worth the hundred dollars I paid to get in. The cashier, a short lady with brown hair who looked bored, glared at me on the way out. I worried that I might see her again, but in a legitimate venue and she'd look at me, pointing and whispering to her friends, telling them, "that guy is pure filth." In daylight, I would tell myself, I was respectable and highly educated and she must be trash working at a place like that. Anything I could tell myself to make that darker version of me seem okay.

I stumbled along the streets of SOMA. Van Ness Avenue was as wide as a riverbed and empty, suffering a drought of cars. I trotted across the road, waiting for something, like getting caught in the crossfire of a drug deal gone bad, stabbed by a hooker or a mad homeless derelict, or struck by a drunk driver. But nothing dark ever happened on those streets.

Or maybe nothing was dark to me anymore. Or I was too scared to go to the places where I really might get hurt. I slid into Christopher's loft where I was poaching space for a couple of months. Christopher, his girlfriend, and the other poacher were all asleep, thinking the night had ended with that final drink in the bar, those last hugs, handshakes, and laughs. I pulled the covers over my eyes. It would be morning soon and my mother's son was something like a whore, a street urchin, or a maggot.

*

Josh and I were walking up Mission Street. It was late. We could hear the echoes of the evening: drunks crawling home, cars parking and unparking themselves, and lights laughing off. The real drunks—the street folk—gathered around the edges of curbs and slid onto corners. Down the block a gunshot rang out and a bunch of guys ran to the other side of the street.

Oh shit, we said. *That's crazy.*

We cut up 20th to Valencia where things were less dicey.

Josh worked at a bar that was too expensive for our friends. All of the drinks were top shelf and beers started at 10 dollars. I would go there looking a bit tattered and get drunk on his employee discount. I would filter into the crowd, full of rich patrons. There were imposters there too. The imposters put the tabs on their credit cards. Josh wore black shoes and liked his job because it wasn't the sort of thing most of his friends did. He was an artist and he worked at an upscale bar. Later he would work as a writer on a popular television show. But before that, before his success, he wrote stories and when he tired of stories he wrote lengthy nonfictions—philosophies and reflections of the people around him, and the telephone poles, and the bus cables that ran a network across the city 14 feet above our heads. And he even wrote about the birds that sat on the cables, talking to each other like the drug dealers on the stoops of the low-income projects around which developers unveiled nouveau-riche neighborhoods.

The gunshot on Mission Street had rattled us slightly. We walked north, away from the Mission and all the way across town to the Marina and the bay. A couple of hours later, rich grapefruit slices of sunlight opened up across the bay and we watched men jump into the water with wet suits—out for morning swims, training for triathlons before work. We took the 22-Fillmore back to our side of town and I remembered a girl Josh had been with. Years ago we had gone to her house for a party and he had found her in a bedroom with another man. He left the house with precision—anger on his face—not as if he had been hurt but as if his calculations for an equation had proven erroneous, as if a closer proofread would have rendered the situation differently. He was disappointed in himself, not her. He brooded for two years and then we heard that gunshot and saw the sunrise by the bay. He left for Los Angeles with a new lover he had met at the upscale bar. She was freer, less of an East Coast equation. She was all West Coast with magnolia smiles and twinkling eyes. She made crafts with her hands and painted pictures of rock musicians and the birds that sat on the cables 14 feet above her head. They married and a year later she left him. He remained on the television show, which, although being a spin-off of another show, had become quite popular on its own and when I last saw him he wasn't drinking anymore. He was sure of himself and the look on his face suggested that he wasn't the one making errors in the equations; rather the women had been the wrong variables, foolishly slipping into his complex romantic theorems, entirely out of their league. Each of us walked with our own seemingly foolproof logic, expecting the rest of the world to understand and obey the rules of our perspectives. But it was each one of us that would need to adapt to or be crushed by the motion of life.

I descended from the 22-Fillmore. It was maybe nine or ten in the morning and I was just getting to bed. A roommate might have shaken his head at me and laughed. I just held tight to the covers and curved around my pillow like a lover, happy that my windows only looked upon the walls of other buildings.

*

It would happen every six weeks or so. Always on a weekend. I would be out with Gavin and Nick and we'd get the phone call. The caller ID would read: HAYDEN. I'd look at it and smile and then show it to Gavin and Nick. They'd laugh and shake their heads as if to say: *Oh shit.*

We would arrive at Hayden's and his girlfriend would be happy and strung out. We'd all get hugs and people would be spread across the floor, sweating like the drug addicts you see in the movies. There would be knolls of cocaine on the table and mason jars full of weed—Hayden pacing around the kitchen, rolling coke around in a sifter like he was a chef at Chez Panisse.

We sat on the floor, listening to John Coltrane or The Velvet Underground. We talked about the latest issue of *The Economist* and the United States' invasion of Iraq. We took sides, someone playing the devil's advocate positing the war's possible merits. Then we spoke of the future and jobs we might have and Nick didn't do any coke. He said, "No thanks, I don't do that, but don't worry, I'm cool with it." He sucked in a big drag of weed. It came out in a dense cloud of smoke. "Once in college," he said, "I lost my mind. I had been up on coke and acid for days and at one point I just cracked, just lost it. I had to step away… But it's cool. You guys carry on. It's cool." His eyes teetered side to side as he talked. I could see desire in those eyes, the hard tug at his will as he worked to hold the line.

I left alone, walking from Hayden's apartment in Russian Hill. It was going to take forever and I had done a line that would carry my legs all the way across town to my bed. I floated over Pine Street, listening to the mechanical chatter of the trolley tracks. They mumbled all of the time, never stopped, like aging, bickering relatives, waiting for something to happen, waiting for a trolley to roll over them. I saw a prostitute on the corner—I had heard they came out at night around there. She was blond or close to blond and her fishnets revealed slim legs. Her red vinyl jacket just barely covered her large bust, which seemed perky in the cool morning air. I was immediately lustful for her but I had to walk because if I stopped walking she would notice me and wonder if I was a john or a cop or a druggie. I saw her face and it was gold. She was the goddess of the block. There wasn't a car in sight or another john on foot. It was as if the girl had been placed there for me. I walked by her, turning right down Pine Street's steep hill toward Polk. I chickened out from contributing to the carnage of human souls—hers, mine, the whole city. It wasn't light outside quite yet but the thick darkness of night had begun to lift and I *knew* people in that neighborhood. Where would we go anyway? I couldn't have her in the apartment.

I grimaced down Polk Street and saw another sex worker but she was different. Crossing over to Polk from Pine, the scene turned into a village of coarse beauties with lipstick, breasts, and cocks. They wore leather around their shoulders and they were never delicate, they were always brutal or rough trade. They didn't have time for people who pretended to be gay. I walked by one, her face black like mine with wisdom and regret.

I asked her, "Are you a real woman?"

She spat at me, "Fuck you, nigga!"

I quickened my pace, that last line of powder lifting me across town like a magical cloud rising from the gutters of bizarro heavens.

During the time I was poaching a corner in his loft, Christopher liked to call me his artist-in-residence, as if he were some great benefactor and I was his charge, like Basquiat toiling away on masterpieces in a basement. Yet, I had no masterpieces and I didn't paint. I was supposed to be a writer but the words refused to obey. Instead, I wrote pieces of songs on Christopher's out-of-tune piano but nothing ever became of them. I played my guitar, enjoying the reverb in the loft. Deep inside, I hoped a melody and a lyric would eventually stick. I needed money, so I flew down to Los Angeles to do a freelance music writing job. I sat in the van of a rock band called Film School that was breaking up or more accurately breaking apart and awaiting reformation in a new version of itself. That's what bands did. They broke up. The players always kept playing. I captured their story on a voice recorder and took notes at a show they played at The Echo in Los Angeles as well as in the van on their way back to San Francisco. They were dissonant to each other. One of them drove, telling jokes only to himself. Another sat shotgun, looking out the window, and another was in his seat, working on a laptop with his headphones, writing new songs for himself, not for the band. The leader and I sat in the back and he smiled oddly, like a king watching the kingdom dissipate in front of his eyes. He didn't give a shit about the crumbling empire. He was older, had been around, and he understood the necessity of dissolution. He was poised to bounce back like an artist in a basement, churning out masterpiece after masterpiece.

*

Gavin and I were looking at each other, wondering what to do. We had beers in front of us and people had packed the bar but that didn't seem like enough. We liked each other because the two of us, we were always looking for something more, something riskier, perhaps something worse. We believed that art was a filthy kernel at the end of a grimy tunnel. Gavin's wide blue eyes held firmly on the glow of the beer in his pint glass. I looked at him and then away. We got a call but it wasn't Hayden. It was Gavin's friend, Mary Ann. She worked in bio-tech and was probably the smartest, kindest person we knew—but she lived in the horrible Marina District and we didn't like going there. That night she wanted us to come over to help finish off her drugs. We had said enough, enough of that kind of stuff. It wasn't getting out of hand but we could see how it might, how it would shift us off the tracks and turn us into caricatures. We didn't want that. We already liked the caricatures we embodied: enlightened art-losers who smoked, drank, and maybe coked but weren't cokeheads. The cab was 15 dollars and that hurt. Mary Ann welcomed us into her clean apartment. Everything was modern and her friends wore Ralph Lauren shirts tucked into khaki pants. There were North Face fleeces strewn on the backs of chairs. She was showing us off. We were her friends from the other side of town. They thought we were rock 'n' roll.

They chattered loudly about finance while putting more of it up their noses. We just watched and smiled and they laughed at us for not doing it. Mary Ann always looking after us, wanting us to be happy in her home—brought us a bottle of Maker's and a bag of pistachios. Gavin and I went back and forth, drinking pinches of whiskey and cracking open the salty nuts. Every time they took long lines up their noses something hurt inside: we wanted it so badly but we didn't want to give in. We wanted to prove to ourselves that we were in control of our lives. We finished the whiskey and smoked a pack of cigarettes. They kept doing lines and laughing about interest rates or maybe even the baseball team and the homerun record. It hurt so bad that Gavin and I started punching each other. The sound—that long *snnIFFF*—killed us, like the siren calls of devils on our shoulders. We found more whiskey and persevered. We were reeling around Mary Ann's apartment, falling over furniture and punching the shit out of each other. A blow connected to my chest and I soared over a couch, tumbling to the floor. Mary Ann tolerated us with poise and dignity, always laughing with warmth, never embarrassed by her rogue friends. We passed out on her couches and while she was high she put covers on us, took off our shoes. All of that whiskey and smoke had taken years off our lives but we woke up and felt fresh for once. We retreated back to the south side of town, ready for brunch or *The New York Times* weekend edition or the park or whatever it is people do on Sundays.

*

We were in Golden Gate, and there was a festival going on around us. It was 10 in the morning and floats filled with fantastically costumed people—some of them nude—rode past us. Gavin and I had pancakes and champagne at his apartment earlier in the morning and now we absorbed the energy of the park. Golden Gate stretched on for a thousand city blocks and everywhere we looked there was nothing but striking mayhem. We had run out of beer and I asked a favor from a kid who was with a group of friends. They wore the uniforms of the Duke University lacrosse team, which was in bad taste as the mostly white team had been accused of raping a black woman in a team house in Durham, North Carolina, that spring. They played their roles so well. The guy told me to fuck off and shoved a beer into my hands. When we wanted some liquor we chased after a float that called itself "Snakes on a Float," which was funny because there had been a movie called *Snakes on a Plane* that had caught popular culture's attention that summer. Like the simple plot of that film—deadly snakes let loose on a plane—there was a bounty of lethal booze on that float. Men and women smiled at us as we chased after it. When we got close enough they poured vodka down our throats. Gavin and I smiled at each other and I knew then that the day would unfold endlessly, that I wouldn't sleep that night and that I'd push myself to the edge of existence and balance my right toe on the tip of a cliff, daring a bastard wind to send me over.

*

I was alone at the Hyde Out when an ex-soldier started talking to me. He began predictably but that didn't make him any less chilling: "It was crazy over there, man. Fucking crazy." I wanted him to like me and I wanted the conversation to ramble on forever so I listened and nodded in earnest. I bought him more drinks when he finished his whiskies and he bought more pints when I finished my beers. "We were in a village, some dipshit of a town. Our guns were out and ready because we knew they were around us in the blown-out holes of windows."

The bartender at the Hyde Out was striking—blond hair and green eyes. She always spoke in calming tones, she listened to my uneven chatter, and she smiled, knowing her smile could make any one of her customers feel better than the condition with which they had arrived. She told me she was going to be an actress. Wrong town, I thought to myself. But when I spoke aloud I encouraged her to push forward with the dream, to place herself center-stage in dramas that would move us to tears, and to become a starlet of the silver screen, a well-dressed icon of our generation.

Sometimes when I came to that bar alone she wasn't there. My heart would sink a bit and another bartender, not as alive, not as filled anymore with such wondrous dreams, would serve me up whiskey and beer. I had come so far from my side of town that I couldn't give up and walk home. I wanted to be a beautiful loser. That bar was full of unknowns and I wanted to be part of their family. Anyone could talk to anyone, young to old, sane to crazy, or sober to drunkard.

Smoking cigarettes with the bartender outside in the mild fog, I would look around the avenue and remember my first days in town when I spent time in the fancier bars of Nob Hill. I was clean-cut back then, the product of a prep school chopping block. But time took away my architecture and I turned into a sticky, knowing ooze that slid through the fault lines of an uncertain future.

"It happened like a fucking lightning bolt, like a missile out of the sky. My buddy went down. There was a bullet in his neck and I was holding him. The blood just kept coming out and I was over the edge. I left him there, I left everyone behind and I tracked down that sniper. I was full of rage. I got into position and unloaded into a hole in a building window. No one else on our team went down so I knew the sniper was dead or hurt bad. When I went in there to shoot him some more I saw that he was a kid, maybe 13 years old. I couldn't shoot him again. I just held him in my arms and that's the first time, the whole time I was over there that I cried. That's the day I gave up, after all those years and all that work, I just gave up."

When I looked into the ex-soldier's eyes all I saw were the remnants of a detonation. We bought more drinks for each other and we touched hands to arms, as close and sentimental as we could get with him being a soldier and me being an unknown.

"I'm here now," he said. "Live right up the street. I paint all day long then come down here to talk to you. Or him. Or her."

*

I talked to another soldier but he wasn't an ex. He was still in action. His name was Cash and he was Christopher's brother. He was a Ranger and his work sent him to the nucleus of the war. The combat-jack, Cash told us, was when a soldier took a few moments off from fighting to get himself off. With bullets cruising through the air, there he is in his dusty hole and he's got his cock out dripping desert cum all over himself. It seemed reasonable to me.

Cash wanted to stop dallying in small talk about the war and get off the couch, get out of his brother's loft, go hit the streets, get drunk and wile some woman into his arms. He was in between tours and the break wasn't long enough to relax from the images of bodies that had piled up on his watch. He had to fill his bloodstream with toxins, both real and metaphorical, turning the trip back home into one large blur, a chaotic dream before awaking to desert missions executed with utter precision and tight-lipped secrecy. Someone picked up a copy of *The New York Times* and remarked at the cover story—there was a bunch of soldiers in a blown-up town and a headline about some minor victory—"I didn't know the Australians were involved in this mess too."

"Well," Cash said, "they might be, but that picture there, those aren't Australians: those are our boys wearing Aussie stripes."

Christopher looked at his brother uneasily. He was happy to see him but he didn't want him to binge. Perhaps he wished they were kids again, trading the frisbee back and forth and dipping headfirst into the Pacific Ocean. I wasn't getting any writing done so I was happy to indulge Cash. I knew we would go out and drink ourselves into a situation. Just then, a cliché fell out of his mouth: "Man, I've been out of the field for a while. I can feel myself getting soft."

I looked at him, a rock of a man, a chiseled superhero. He surveyed the city's bars, often courting women who were distinguished products of higher education in bourgeois attire. He culled them into concise romantic encounters and he would be gone before they woke up. A story leaked that while on R&R, Cash had beaten up people near his fort in Georgia and then driven a car so drunk that the police were more mystified with his ability to maneuver the vehicle than angry with his violation of the law. And later, there were stories about him controlling groups of women like platoons, sending some of them out on missions to get him food, laundry, and newspapers while he slept with others. He seemed to vacillate between the perverse desire to control everything and the nihilistic resignation to control nothing at all. I hadn't been to war but in his eyes I could glean a flickering shadow of my own reflection.

Christopher told me he'd be in bed each night, worrying if his brother would ever be the same. I said he'd be okay but I should have told Christopher to be more honest. The truth was as clear as a director's dailies: his brother, as likeable and charming as he was, would be projecting a horror film for the rest of his life.

*

I was in New York for three days. My friends had scattered about the city—the artists and liberals in Williamsburg, the frontiers-men in Long Island City, and the financiers on the Upper East Side. I bounced around the boroughs, trying to learn how they saw the world. I met up with a friend who had just returned from Thailand. He worked for a colossal financial institution downtown. This was before the Great Recession. We sat in a rundown bar just a few blocks away from the towers of finance and investment. He said, "This is where all of the bankers come for burgers and beers during work." The burgers were huge and I found it difficult to wrap my hand around the large cups of cheap beer we were drinking. My friend had returned from the field, deeply embedded in Bangkok. He was not unlike Cash who had made his way back to home-base after his work in Iraq; only Cash traded in bullets and my friend traded in speculation.

"Let's go," he said. "Or we'll be late for our appointment."

We walked back to his office, back to work, the hazy effects of the cheap beer pulsing through my head. I presented my identification and signed a thick stack of papers to get into his company's building. We went several stories up into the air. My friend dropped his bag by his office and, after looking at me curiously, he adjusted the collar of my button-down shirt. We got back on the elevator, went up a few more floors, and got off. We walked over to another elevator, a special-issue model. The door was open and an operator stood there, a gray-haired black man, maybe 65 years old. He wore a suit but not an executive's suit, rather the kind of suit someone in service wears so that it is always clear who commands and who obeys. "Gentlemen," he said, "you're right on time."

We got in the elevator and he took us up a few more flights. He let us off and said, "I will be back in 15 minutes to take you back down."

The door closed behind us.

We were at the top of the building. My friend led me into the special room. It was so special that he had to schedule an appointment just to get us access. Fifteen minutes and not everyone even got that. I spun around, astonished. The room was cylindrical and its walls were windows that wrapped around the length of the entire space. We could see all of New York— every borough, every building, every detail. The expanse of the great city was before us and like accidental explorers we could see the vast spoils of the land, all within our reach. In the center of the room was a large rotating globe made of silver or platinum—something magnificent. Now the entire Earth sat in front of us. I stared at the globe, amazed and transfixed. My friend walked over to it and gave a hearty push. North America spun by, then Asia, then Africa. "This," he said, "is where the rich white men decide how they will divvy up the world." He laughed loudly, his voice echoing, filling up the room.

I was glad I had seen it. I was glad that I knew.

*

I kept writing but the words eluded meaning. I couldn't understand myself so how was I to understand the world? For all of my privileges I felt vacant and broken. Despite this fog, new songs took form and I played a show at the Hemlock Tavern on Polk Street. Friends from past and present gathered 'round to see me, to see each other, and to begin the weekend. If it had happened in black-and-white then it would have been a film, the closing scene that walks us out of the woods to show that the masks we wear aren't faces we can ever lose: someday we will have to wear them again or at least look at their faded and crinkled edges and realize they are just layers of skin we peeled away. If my parents had been there and had the first girl I ever fell in love with been there too, it would have been a Hollywood ending. But really, my movements are just endless episodes of a television show: slight changes in setting spliced against unforgettable, unshakeable patterns.

I saw Hayden and was happy to see him. He seemed clean and sharp, back on his feet with a modest cocktail in his hand. He had broken up with his girlfriend and other habits had left with her; though he did look a little pained and distant for choosing to live the straight life.

I played the show. Men and women shook my hand and hugged me. Everyone bought drinks. Amidst the swell of excitement, I snuck away, exiting my own dream, and converged with a familiar clutch of characters at a separate engagement on the south side of town.

We were at Gavin's and Nick was there. There were women and men laughing and drinking wine. We listened to The Clash and I got close to a woman who had dated a rich friend of mine, a guy who always came to see me whenever I got it together to play a show. He was probably still at the show. She was sweating and we kissed. I wanted less to love her than for her to just give me someone or something to wake up to. And then there was Nick. He no longer told us the story about losing his mind at the end of college, he just said: *cut me a line and make it fucking big.* I was briefly dizzy and a feeling came over me, one of these moments I have from time to time. It occurred to me that there was nothing that had changed except my age. I was still black. I was still lost. Even to myself I was an invisible man.

I started to say something aloud to the group, but caught myself and pushed forward into the slippery cavity of the girl's mouth.

American Gray Space

1

"Nigger music," he said.

He paused and thought deeply for a moment. "Yeah, that's what we do: full on nigger music. It's fucking great."

I wasn't quite sure what to say so I leaned into the couch and mumbled something like, "That sounds fascinating. I've got to come see that sometime."

San Francisco hipsters filled the corners of the dark apartment. Outside, a light rain came down around the city. Conversations oscillated between fashion and music. I could have talked to so many people but I had chosen this skinny musician who had tried to French kiss me earlier. In that moment, he seemed like a true artist to me—someone who created, revised, destroyed, and rebuilt in an effort to understand the world. And, he played nigger music. Was it a travesty or a triumph that this skinny, five-o'clock-shadowed white guy had so comfortably described his band's style of music to me, a skinny, five-o'clock-shadowed black guy, as none other than "nigger music"? He apparently didn't know what else to call it. He said that his rock band, Mutilated Mannequins, constructed lyrical diatribes on racism, pairing them with gripping art-rock freak-outs. He was so sincere, calm, and honest. His eyes homed in on me, his confidence unwavering. His philosophies unfolded: "We are doing important shit, man. Rethinking the whole world. The whole fucking paradigm."

He went on describing his music. After some time his words echoed listlessly like the distant pitter-patter of rain on the windowsill. I thought about punching him in the neck. I was in a state of existential shock. Lifting up from my body I considered that I needed to spend less nights like this: 26 years old, going to work, making music, barely sleeping, and then going out just to hear someone talk about nigger music. The enduring question lingered: would it ever be possible for a non-black person to throw around the word *nigger* in a non-malicious sense? Does the weight of such a word truly vary with context or is it a shotgun shell whenever it gets fired into the air? And, damn, sometimes it takes a minute to figure out how they're shooting. Former NAACP representative Julian Bond said that the 2nd Civil Rights Movement will be harder because the "Whites Only" signs have been taken down. Yet their shadows remain firmly placed to doorways and water fountains. How do you challenge a ghost when you can't even touch it?

I visited the University of Virginia when I was 19. I was a freshman studying at Princeton but I joined some friends for a road trip. The campus stood as a memorial to Thomas Jefferson— political leader, slave owner, and sexual violator. I stumbled down fraternity row, drunk and foggy, beneath a warm blanket of Gentleman Jack Daniel's. I had chased down the whiskey with half a case of Natural Light. Then I had lost my friends at the Delta Kappa Epsilon fraternity house. That was the place where they tossed couches from the second-floor balcony when they got bored.

I had spent the day tracking down friends from D.C. In high school, our class was so small that there wasn't much room for segregation. White kids and the rest of us spent a lot of time together—we were mostly all friends. Yet, just several months removed from that privileged prep school experience, I found that all of my friends had splintered into different circles in Charlottesville. If they did not see each other because of their different academic and social interests, I could understand that, but the realization that white and black people did not congregate socially at such a distinguished school shocked me. I had been fast asleep and suddenly I was awake. As I grew older and more explicitly understood the context in which the University of Virginia had been conceived, it was my early-college naivete that would prove more shocking. It is a school and community that pays homage to a remarkable, elite, and intelligent hero, Thomas Jefferson, who, in the midst of his accomplishments, embraced the ownership—and sexual predation—of slaves toward his own benefit. The system, from its inception, was complex and cracked.

As the evening descended, I conspired to find my college friends whom I had parted from earlier. In an age before cell phones, I asked a group of white-shirt, dark-tie frat boys sitting on the steps of another fraternity if they had seen about four or five guys in Princeton t-shirts walking by.

One of them stepped forward, stars and bars glistening behind his eyes, and pointed in a direction that I had no intention of following. He said, "A bunch of black guys came by here 10 minutes ago. They went that way."

He might have been helpful had I specifically inquired about black friends, but I hadn't and his assumptions bred something foul in my stomach. He had used the golden sword of 21st century racists. He had called me a nigger without even using the word. The invisible noun: it just needs to be insinuated—a subtle threat of a bomb that could go off at any moment. I waved my hand at him, pushing away his advice, a dismissal of what he had to offer. I could have taken them on. I could have traded in bloody teeth for intangible pride. I could have found out if they have "Whites Only" signs in Valhalla.

2

Wait, do you remember the first time you put that record on? Maybe it was a CD or a tape. My roommate had picked up the LP from a San Francisco street vendor for 99 cents: Elvis Costello's 1978 album *This Year's Model*. That picture on the front is priceless: Elvis bent over a camera, taking a picture of you, turning the listener into his model. The album's third track, "The Beat," captures the essence of new wave music as well as Blondie, The Cars, and Talking Heads had done in entire albums. I used to spin "The Beat" and other songs off *This Year's Model* at late-night house parties just when the makeshift dance floor of someone's apartment needed one more momentous lift. That song, no, that whole album, was always reliable. I even owned the CD, the expanded edition with all of the demos and b-sides.

One day a friend told me the old story about Elvis Costello calling Ray Charles a "blind, ignorant nigger" during a drunken argument with Bonnie Bramlett and Stephen Stills in a Columbus, Ohio, bar in 1979. When I heard the story, my blood froze up like Arctic pistons. I stopped listening to Costello immediately. Listening to his music would have felt like a betrayal to my identity, my people. I leafed through numerous articles on the Internet, detailing Costello's frequent attempts to reckon with and apologize for the incident. Costello, whose actions have often put him on the side of peace, social justice, and equality, has witnessed the weight of his words follow him into his golden years—as recently as 2015 he discussed and apologized for his drunken, youthful missteps in an interview with ?uestlove. Even though I wouldn't listen to him, I couldn't bring myself to throw out his albums. I was caught somewhere between my love for the music and a mistake that I couldn't forgive. *This Year's Model* remains tucked away in my long shelf of vinyl.

Mick Jagger famously referred to black women as "brown sugar" in a song of the same name, then managed to squeeze out a phrase about "ten little niggers sittin' on da wall" in "Sweet Black Angel"—confusingly in a song about civil rights activist Angela Davis—and came full-circle with the revelation that "black girls just wanna get fucked all night long" on 1978's "Some Girls," a song that disparaged women of all backgrounds.

Nevertheless, there was a period when I listened to the Stones all of the time and something about it killed me. Why should Costello get the sanction while the Stones have access to my stereo? Maybe their oft-professed debt to black musicians excuses their racial errs. *Wait, Costello loves black American music.* Perhaps it's the fact that they have been roundly sexist, racist, and offensive to practically everyone on Earth. *But Costello appears to be one of the nicest people in the music industry.* It certainly must be their combination of irresistible hooks, intriguing decadence, and unapologetic rock 'n' roll clichés that make them the bad guys that I hate to love. *Isn't "Alison" one of the catchiest pieces of pop ever written?*

Rap artists Mobb Deep's second album, *The Infamous*, is one of the best albums of the last century. It offers a gritty portrayal of New York life, possessing a distinct literary honesty akin to Lou Reed's impressions of the city through his solo work and albums with The Velvet Underground. If I dared to count the number of times they throw out the n-word on that album, I would find myself needing a secretary. But why would I count? Their n-bombs and tales of urban violence don't bother me when I'm listening to the music. Even though they had art-school backgrounds, their drug-lord sound is so convincing that it doesn't matter. And who is to say drug lords can't be artists? When I think about Mobb Deep and their *Infamous* album, and really, any number of rap albums can serve as the control here, my reasonable side tells me that I should be bothered by their loose use of *nigger*—trap talk and misogyny aside. But it sounds so good.

I catch myself in the car or listening to music on my phone, rattling off lines like, "This nigga that I'm beginning to dislike, he got me fed/If he doesn't discontinue his bullshit, he might be dead," as if they were my own.

Rap producer Dr. Dre makes records that millions of people can dance and bob their heads to. He's been doing it for years through the voices of a variety of rappers: Ice Cube, Snoop Dogg, Eminem, Kendrick Lamar. He is a legend. Yet he was also a member of a band called N.W.A—Niggaz with Attitudes—and produced an album called *Niggaz4Life*. Does he feel at this point in his career, when he can roll up to the Grammy Awards, looking dapper and decidedly un-gangsta, that he is a nigger for life? This is the man who co-founded Beats Audio, a company purchased by Apple for several billion dollars. Or does no amount of corporate wealth and industry success protect a luminary even like Dr. Dre?

Perhaps in the entertainment world it doesn't matter what you call yourself as long as you manufacture hits for the executives. *Good reviews from the critics are a plus, but only optional.* And if to Dr. Dre and others, the "nigga4life" lifestyle means casual sex, getting high, and flaunting money, then perhaps it can be a black term for *rock star*; in which case, Keith Richards, Tommy Lee, and Dave Navarro all could have had guest spots on the *Niggaz4Life* album.

How does the rest of the country consider Dr. Dre? How might a white rap-listening college graduate working on Capitol Hill feel about a rap icon? Does this white college grad consider the image of the African American portrayed in hip-hop when considering larger racial issues? Or does he even care to mix his art with politics and ethics? Maybe after all it's *just* music and the ethos of rock 'n' roll filtered through the African American experience comes out in such a way that niggers are homies are bros are pals are dudes are your crew. What are the nationwide effects if everyone, not just black people, buys into this logic?

Or is it already selling? Rap music rarely goes multi-platinum without white money. So where are the white listeners—the ones who roll down the street en route to middle-class jobs in their trucks, shaking the whole block with the bass and rhymes of A$AP Rocky, Rick Ross, and The Game—where are they when it is time to stand in the streets for justice, for the requiems of Sandra Bland, Michael Brown, and the ever-expanding roll call of innocent lives consumed by hate? Where are they when they just need to vote for the right person? To have it both ways, for all of us, is a distinct privilege that we should never invoke.

3

My brother, a successful lawyer, was sitting in a Dunkin' Donuts in a suburb of Boston with his two-and-a-half-year-old daughter. He assumed a high school football game was going on nearby when a group of teenage African American males walked into the shop and raised a little bit of juvenile hell. No, not guns and threats, just loud voices and lewd conversation: universal adolescent behavior. An older white man asked them to keep it down and one of them rallied back, "What's the matter, don't you have a real Dunkin' Donuts in your neighborhood?" As my brother began to pack up his things the boys left the shop. The manager, who my brother assumed to be Indian or Pakistani, promptly called the police.

My brother left before the police came but he relayed two thoughts to me over the phone. The first: why did those kids have to be so inappropriately unruly—don't they know the camera is always unfairly turned on them as young black bodies? The second: why the hell did the manager call the police? What were the police going to do? Nothing had *really* happened. No guns were pulled and no one was assaulted—though in this current era, such an encounter could have resulted in death. My brother felt burned by the kids for shaking the fragile image of black Americans and offended by the overreaction from the store manager. He hadn't done anything. He had just shown up for donuts and coffee. And that old white man, what exactly did he think? Did he see two different types of people in his mind or were the rowdy kids and my brother cut from the same rock?

From Kaplan's popular study guide, The Real GRE: Surviving the American Social Landscape

The New New Analogy

Directions: Pick the best answer and then write an explanation for the answer you choose. If you are having difficulty forming your thoughts then read the sample answers provided below.

NIGGER : BLACK PERSON ::
A. TYPE A : TYPE B
B. PAST : FUTURE
C. INFERIOR : SUPERIOR
D. PART : WHOLE
E. ALL ANSWERS ARE CORRECT

Sample Answers:

TYPE A : TYPE B
Rapper Lil Jon grew up in a stable middle-class environment. Will Smith did as well. Both entertainers are smart and successful and their professional end-goals run parallel: amassing significant amounts of wealth; but Will Smith has moved down a path that has allowed him to sustain a black identity

without being stereotyped as ghetto or gangster. He moves seamlessly between different performances, from pairing with Martin Lawrence in the action-comedy *Bad Boys* to working with Donald Sutherland in the art-house theatrics of *Six Degrees of Separation* to big-screen science fiction blockbusters like *Men in Black*. White people love Will Smith. They buy tickets to his movies. In contrast, Lil Jon has cashed in on a more street-level aesthetic, less concerned with established "etiquette" or playing it both ways. In the early 2000s, Lil Jon called his Southern blend of hip-hop "crunk." With genre classics like "Real Nigga Roll Call" and "Move Bitch," it sold a lot of units. Without seeing the market reports, it is safe to assume that black rap fans weren't the only ones picking up these records. Again, it takes white American dollars for records to go platinum. White people loved Lil Jon. They bought copies of his records. They consumed his reflection of life· as a never-ending gangsta-party.

PAST : FUTURE

Q-Tip, the talented rapper from A Tribe Called Quest, considered the n-word's history and the politics of its use within black culture in "Sucka Nigga" — the meditation so important that he raps the same verse twice. The song ends with a vocal sample that refers to the use of the n-word, denoting, "You're not any less of a man if you don't pull the trigger/ You're not necessarily a man if you do." In his own practice as a rapper, Q-Tip has both used the word, over the years, in a number of different ways, sometimes critiquing aspects of African American culture and at other times as a term of endearment. In "Sucka Nigga" he raps, "Yo I start to flinch as I try not to say it/But my lips is like the oowop as I start to spray it." Both the embrace and the regret are palpable as Q-Tip attempts to walk the tight-rope of this heavy cultural question. By putting off his termination of the word in his lyrics, is Q-Tip acting a bit like our founding fathers: at the birth of our nation they decided to hold off on solving the problem of slavery, even though they knew it was an issue that would eventually have to be dealt with. Who forms a republic based on equality and freedom and also has slaves?

INFERIOR : SUPERIOR

Chris Rock, in his stand-up comedy special *Bring the Pain*, remarked about a civil war occurring within the black community. He said there was a war between black folks and niggers. Via the hard binary of his perspective: black folks represented reasonable American citizens while niggers reflected an approach of playing outside of the rules of day-to-day life in American society. It still stands as one of the most public and accessible essays on oft-discussed rifts within the black American community. By using the terms *blacks* and *niggers* he immediately identified a class issue within the community — the difference in class being: are you capable of acting in a way that is deemed acceptable by Western societal standards — i.e., the identity-crushing step toward assimilation — or will you choose an alternate path, and forever be kept on the perimeter? Are these the only two choices?

PART : WHOLE

As much as Chris Rock suggests that niggers are inferior to black people, by using the Civil War analogy he is also suggesting that they are part of a greater whole. And whether it was intentional or not, Rock's "joke" about the class structure of the black community applies to all Americans: class is an all-American issue. Each ethnic, religious, and social group is made up of a number of different parts that comprise the whole. After all, what would upstanding white people be without their white trash? They would all just be white — and it would be impossible for white people to define success within their own ranks if someone wasn't stereotypically getting drunk and knocking up their cousin in the trailer park. How socially successful can a professional black man or woman be if some other black person isn't around to tip the tables of ignorance? Human class structure requires us to draw these lines — and so often one's class is determined by their birth right. So how can black Americans fight the powers that be and still be human?

He played guitar and the name of his band was Mutilated Mannequins. They played nigger music. I am black and always looking for answers. I had no choice but to track them down.

On a foggy Saturday night I squeezed my way through the crowded bar of Edinburgh Castle in San Francisco's Tender-Nob neighborhood. Hipsters swelled around the bar, ordering up Newcastle, High Life, and Guinness, throwing back Irish car bombs and cleaning up shots of whiskey. I came in uniform—the slightly torn blue jeans, the frayed prep-school sweater, and a scarf that identified me as a thinking man's hipster rather than a downtown, flophouse art-school casualty. Beer in hand, I stormed upstairs, alone and on a mission to see the Mannequins play their music, to convince me of their perverse Afro-centric cause.

The band's three members looked so intentionally special with their '80s lipstick and clothes tighter than the bodies they struggled and sometimes failed to cover. On first listen, the music didn't seem so much like black music or music at all. Rather it came off like a grating performance-art headache. Melodies were scarce and lyrics were rendered indecipherable underneath the screams and bellows of the singer's anguish. My "friend," who played guitar and tried to kiss me at a late-night party while telling me that his band played "nigger music," loomed in a corner of the stage, bursting into epileptic theatrics from time to time. The keyboardist humped a synthesizer with his fists and occasionally pushed buttons on a drum machine.

Despite the noisy fuss, the singer was visually captivating: he was black with dreadlocks, all done-up with beautiful glam makeup, positively gay, loud, and possessed.

he sang: *Caucasian neocolonist/Wanting to freak with the freakest/Seeking and searching for the scariest/Thugged out nigga pussy terrorist.* **and he shouted:** *Welcome to the plantation/We the niggas sexing the nation/White folk, white folk be giving ovation like head/I guess we quite the sensation.*

I talked to him for a bit after the show but in person he was much too art-scenester and I was too much of an indie-prepster; even our shared blackness and interest in music wasn't enough to make us want to hang out for more than five minutes. Yet from that night on, every time I saw him tucked into the corners of a San Francisco bar with a lover in his arm, we always nodded to each other—that ever-bonding "black man nod" to acknowledge: yes, I see you, brother, and even though I'm wearing a skinny tie and listening to New Order and you're walking off with your analyst colleagues to a power lunch, I still got your back because, shit, we're black, and this shit is real from backalleys to boardrooms.

I was intrigued by the motions of the Mutilated Mannequins' singer if not by his band's sounds. They pushed some cultural buttons from behind their wall of noise. Their lyrics attacked American racial issues head-on. Yet, I left the show feeling a little bit unsatisfied. They buried their diatribe under the noise. A passive listener could have missed it. I wondered and couldn't quite determine why the singer had given license to his arty white friends to play and promote his nigger music. I didn't want to listen to his friends as much as I wanted to read what he had to say. Perhaps he was afraid to state his case in such plain terms or maybe he was trying to represent the true nature of the race issue in America: a wealth of ideas covered up by white noise—screaming to be heard. And if it was nigger music then it was also American music

I left the clamor of the Edinburgh Castle, walking back onto the streets of the Tenderloin where drinking, poverty, and drugs all converged. I moved into the night, continuing to run my fingers across the gray-skinned canvas on which many of our country's stories are painted.

Installations

So, we had to leave the apartment because there were bed bugs. And also the band had broken up. I think the band broke up first and then we found the bed bugs. Either way they were both crushing blows. The band had become our life or our identity and the apartment was the central nervous system from which we had dispatched our movements to the rest of the world around us.

I had seen the first bug. It was on the side of my mattress and I gasped, virtually soiled my pants. It all felt terrible and weird and also kind of cool because it was like a Henry Miller book in Paris with libertines and expatriates and crabs and bugs and I, too, wanted to be a writer so it seemed like a rite of passage. I thought, perhaps, that I was living the degenerate yet romantic underbelly life of an artist. We traced the bugs back to a Halloween party we had thrown and a transient stoner who had ended up crashing at our place. She had slept in my room, hoping for a sign, I think, but I had lain there all night, frozen on my side of the bed, too nervous to ask her to sleep on the couch. Those awkward facts deflated a bit of the dark romance of living in the city, close to the edge, with libertines and bugs, but still, the writer in me thought I had progressed to a new level of literary cool. Even after the exterminator came and killed them, we had to leave. It just didn't seem right to stay and how could we—with the band in pieces and ex-members dispatching to new adventures? Plus, we couldn't sleep at night. Even with the bugs gone I'd teeter on the edge of insanity, wondering if that itch at the bottom of my ankle was just a benign scratch or the fierce incisors of a vampire creature gnawing at my flesh.

We lived in San Francisco. For all of us it had been a new home, an escape from Northeastern expectations and the hectic call of New York. We had found our feet in this new town. We were young, somewhat adventurous, and we played in rock bands, which seemed at the time, like a great way to say, no, we will not follow your rules. But now we were broken, shifting from identities we had gripped onto: late nights in clubs with tight jeans, beers, and guitars, approximating how we might look cool. Or perhaps I should speak for myself. I wanted to look cool. I wanted to be the artist. I was the one escaping from something back East, some intangible shroud that cast itself over my heart, hoping to pull me back to the coast with sharp ties around my neck, oxfords on my shoulders, and khakis on my legs. But I wouldn't go—even if I had been displaced, by bed bugs no less, in my adopted West Coast home.

Our apartment sat at the crowded intersection of Church and Market Streets in the heart of the city's nightlife, a point where the edges of various districts—the lower Haight, the Mission, and Castro—all merge. We had chosen the place because we could fit all of our instruments into one of the living rooms and we could play late into the night. We each paid rent of roughly 600 a month and that meant we could work our jobs, make our art, and still exist in the city. My new neighborhood, only a few blocks away and a bit deeper into the Mission, was quiet in comparison. I would miss the energy of this place. People were always floating through our hallways and living rooms and kitchen. I'd come home from work and there would be a commune of people out on our deck, charring fresh salmon and corn on the grill, drinking cold bottles of Pacifico with plump limes stuffed into the necks. Or sometimes we'd come home from the bars and there would be a party in our apartment that none of us had organized.

Outside, the streets were alive with incessant, echoing chatter. The people moved in and out of buildings, cafés, and restaurants.

Even the cars spoke and the buses sighed as they came to a halt at the intersection and the cables above the buses buzzed with electric hearts.

The neighborhood's peculiarities had glued themselves to my persona: the average yet serviceable diner across the street, ready to cook me burgers or eggs at any hour, or Aardvark, the used bookstore a few storefronts down from us where I could barter with the tall gray-haired beatnik behind the counter about the prices of the books I wanted to buy and sell. The bar next door, Pilsner Inn, was a popular gay bar and on the weekends its party-forward energy spilled from the center of the bar onto the sidewalk. When we first moved to the block, years ago when we were all in the band together, when our dream of the band and living in the city was more important than any professional metric of success, I spent solitary hours in the Pilsner. I wasn't gay but I liked being there, drinking a whiskey alone, passing for a few moments, allowed to step out of my own identity and try someone else's skin. It was one of the lures of the city, to be someone else or not even worry about who you were: to forget about yourself, to be alone in the company of others with their eyes not even watching or caring about you.

I tried to plan ahead for the move. Weeks in advance I gathered boxes and put belongings into neat piles. I sold records I didn't listen to anymore. I whittled down my wardrobe, selling some of it and giving the rest of it away to charity—God forbid there were any remaining little bug eggs in the folds of those collared shirts, waiting to hatch and tear apart the necks and ankles of unsuspecting victims. I shredded useless documents and financial histories. I tried to do it all but still I stood there, sweaty and tired, facing the inevitable truth that moving breaks us, through sheer physical and spiritual exhaustion, and there is little we can do to ease the pain.

All afternoon, I had been carrying items from the front gate of the apartment to the van I had rented, a half-block down the street. My older brother, who was helping out, stood by the van with a Black Dog cap, sipping a cup of coffee and guarding my wares. We took three trips from my old apartment to the new place. By the last trip I was worn out, lying on my new hardwood floor, surrounded by boxes. Had I really succeeded after all? It seemed that even after cutting loose half my belongings I was still crouching under skyscrapers of debatable essentials. I got a call from two of my soon-to-be former roommates... bandmates. They were wondering when I'd be over to clean out the old place. There was no sign of our fourth roommate, they said, so it would just be the three of us. The one who was missing had broken up our band.

We had a handful of Coronas left in the fridge and they kept us loose as we fixed up the place. We had also left behind stacks of various items that no one wanted to take. There was an old boxy pre-flat-screen television, a couple of CRT computer monitors, an L-shaped couch perfect for a dorm room, a few footstools, and a kitchen full of food. One of the roommates decided that we would simply take everything down to the busy street corner and let the passing scavengers have at it. He began with the quality goods, taking the television and the couch down first, placing them right in front of a gleeful audience of drinkers who were sitting at the Pilsner Inn. It was a Saturday afternoon and the bar folk were already tight and raucous. They cheered and cooed at us when we brought down more stuff. As the items piled up, barflies emerged from their den. In time, our belongings disappeared from our curbside market. A hipster couple in matching skin-tight jeans pored over the couch. I wondered how their skeletal frames would manage to carry it back home. My old computer desk was gone before I could head back up the stairs. I couldn't believe it; I hated that thing. Some Dutch engineer had designed it to punish me during its assembly. But as a fully assembled floor model it was gone in an instant. Once we liquidated the major appliances, we began working through our kitchen and bagging up food. We had glass bottles of seasonings and boxes of pasta. One roommate had cans of Heinz baked beans stored away like wartime rations. We put all of it on the curb and people snatched them up to offer them homes in new pantries.

Our little Church Street market became an event, the sort of spontaneous happening that can only unfold in a city. Our ritual of detachment, of shedding our skin and starting anew had become public kabuki, only our faces were caked in layers of dried sweat rather than white makeup. People on afternoon walks could stop by to see our bazaar and take what they pleased. For the men in the bar we must have seemed like a piece of theater, characters and props moving on and off the stage. Soon we would be gone. People would come home from their walks and eat dinner, perhaps working the sight of our sidewalk marketplace into the greater narrative of their afternoon in the neighborhood or simply discarding it as more noise in a hectic metropolis. Drinkers would leave the bar and go to other bars, perhaps making note of us to their new friends in the new bars or simply forgetting about us, letting us slip away as quickly as the last sips of beer at the bottoms of their pint glasses.

Kicking around the remains of my former bedroom, I came across a couple of books that I had forgotten to pack or sell. There was a museum book about visual artist Eva Hesse and another about finding employment in San Francisco. Both seemed like relics from a forgotten time so I took them down to Aardvark. Every time I walked by the bar, even with a couple of stuffy books under my arm, the clientele would cheer at me, clink their glasses, and knock back a drink.

I walked into the bookstore, thinking I might get some money from the resident gray-haired hippie. But mostly, I was excited to see Wendy, a young woman who worked there. She had dark-red hair, was from Southern California, and seemed, in equal parts, rural, geeky, and goth. She wore black dresses with black jeans underneath and her teeth were cracked and stained. Yet she smiled with pride. Her flaws gave her character. They weren't flaws at all. Every time I saw her in the store, something shook in me, a little tremor in my chest. Wendy's spirit transported me: that smile and her eagerness to talk, laugh, or recommend a book. In moving to San Francisco she had rejected a middling, dead-end existence in Southern California: worn-out friendships and a cheerless future. She had escaped, like the rest of us, from *something*, whatever it was, to find new direction, or to forthrightly clasp onto the *lack* of needing to find a direction. We talked of music and the shows we would see in coming weeks. And we talked of my move but I didn't mention the bed bugs. Wendy didn't need to know about the bugs. Her full beauty was palpable and at the core of the attraction, I think, was our shared certitude in the promise of a new start.

The gray-haired book buyer gave my copy of the Eva Hesse book the once-over. "You know, I think we've already got this."

"Oh really?" I asked.

"Yeah, let me go check."

He walked over to the bookshelf and took out a copy of the same book. My heart sunk a bit. "Hey, just take it for free," I said. "Someone will like it."

He smiled and insisted that I take eight dollars for the book. I took the money and waved goodbye to Wendy. When would I see her again? I wondered. Would I ever ask her out?

It was nighttime and by now the homeless citizens of the streets had taken notice of our belongings on the curb. They found treasures in what the privileged class saw as trash, picking up empty bottles, odd garments, and old magazines. Our apartment neared emptiness, becoming an open space where new people could have a go at life in a buzzing neighborhood, where bugs that had hidden in the deepest crevices and cracks of our walls—rebuilding their base—could launch an offensive on virgin residents. There were a few more things to be patched up but we left them for our absent roommate to take care of whenever he arrived. We decided to celebrate with a big dinner but first I had to make a final trip to my new place, as I had produced new stacks of moveable items. I left to get the van, which was parked a couple of blocks away. Outside of the apartment, I looked around, taking in the busy fervor of Church Street. Noise littered the block but a distant voice called out for me. I ignored it but it kept calling. Finally, I tuned in.

"Hey, is that your stuff?"

I turned around and the gray-haired bookseller was looking at me. "What?"

"Is that all of your stuff?"

He pointed to our dwindling stack of belongings on the sidewalk. I smiled, kind of proud of our urban mess. "Yeah, it's ours, but now it's everybody's."

He turned a bit red. Time stuttered and he began to fume. A boulder formed in my gut. He erupted. "That's wrong. That's fucking wrong! You can't just leave your shit here! You are using the city as your dumpster and it is wrong!"

I was overwhelmed. One of my roommates walked by, shocked to see this older man screaming in the street. The man retreated into the bookstore. I continued to help out with the loading process but I couldn't think straight. My heart was pumping. I wanted to go in the shop and tell him off, but what was the use? I continued packing. A couple of minutes later the bookseller ran back out to the street. He screamed at us—*you assholes*. I saw my roommate tensing up, his fists tightening, getting ready to protect a friend. The man had a book in his hands and he threw it at the back of the van.

"Next time I'll break the window," he yelled. It was the Eva Hesse book. There she was, back in my life, unwilling to be left behind. "I'm going to call the police," he shouted. "This is bullshit!"

I felt my own blood heating, preparing for violence. It was another sort of spontaneous happening that unfolds in city streets. It was the unpredictable turn of weather, a fog that sweeps away a sunny afternoon. It was a moment of repressed anger, an emotion bursting without warning. A thriving city block turns into a minor crime scene as unlikely felons have it out with each other. I kept my exterior calm.

"Please leave us alone," I said.

He walked into the store and picked up the phone. I lingered, wondering what had broken him, pushed him to these furious edges. How long had he held this anger within him? Years? Decades? Was it the memory of a childhood trauma, triggered by something as trivial as leaving a decent couch on the sidewalk for the first lucky taker? Or was it the endless crush of surviving in San Francisco, its hands forming around his heart and slowly squeezing it tighter and tighter every day? As if the act of moving wasn't enough to mash my spirit, it seemed incredible that I would meet such a violent separation from my old neighborhood. Indeed, one of my neighbors was screaming at me, threatening me, and hurling books at me after two years of smiles, salutations, and handshake trades of old literature for new money. I was sad for him and I also wanted to hurt him. Perhaps his fury was the fury of the neighborhood itself, personified and lashing out at my departure through the mouth of this wild man. But the neighborhood couldn't care about me like that. The city is a machine. We cannot fight it or deny it. We can only react to the strange events it offers.

Suddenly, a dense thud, like two juggernauts colliding, erupted from Church Street. Tires screeched and then everything was silent. A street like that never goes silent. I swung around and the picture of the avenue was frozen: small car with a young guy behind the wheel, maybe 21, and, outside, a street wanderer, maybe 60, looking like a dead Willie Nelson. There he was, sprawled out on the pavement, his mind distant, talking with spirits the rest of us couldn't see. I ran across the street and knelt on one side of the man, searching for vital signs. His body was bulging through his black jeans and black leather jacket. It was as if his insides had popped like wild carnival balloons, the air pushing his bones and muscles against the elastic casing of his skin. I thought he was exploding. He was breathing and he reached out for my hand. I held him gently but firm enough so that he knew I was really there. I scrambled for my cell phone with my other hand and began an urgent dialogue with 9-1-1. The man moaned in cat-like yelps. I considered his face and the strange years that had brought him to this concrete deathbed. He looked like a cowboy or a rebel. Had he been in a motorcycle gang in the '60s? Did he run wild across the hills and highways of Northern California with a bottle of whiskey by his side, a switchblade in his hand, and a cigarette in his mouth? Had he been at Altamont and how had the '80s and '90s displaced him? Was he one of the institutionalized that late-'60s California had helped push onto the streets? What fate had carried him through so many chapters and dropped him in my arms? Around us, traffic slowed to a humble and respectful drone. Cars pulled away from the scene, turning off Church Street to make room for the emergency vehicles. The old man's eyes seem black in my memory. His own head must have been full of memories and questions and perhaps even resolution. It seems to me that at some point, in our own way, we all find ourselves spread out on a busy intersection, broken, and looking up at the sky, holding a stranger's hand.

The medics arrived and I let go of him. I fell back from the scene, letting the professionals assume their roles. I sat down on the curb and my eyes settled on the stiff black tar of the street. I slowly returned to the van. My roommates were ready to go. I held up my hand, signaling them to wait a moment. I walked into the bookstore. I was suddenly peaceful. I looked at the book buyer and uttered my words like I was in a self-help class on how to speak with positive language. "If you're upset with me, it's okay. All I ask is that you approach me in an appropriate way."

He fired back, "You're wrong. It's bullshit. I was going to call the cops until…"

The whole bookstore was uncomfortable. No one could leave, browse, or buy anything. "If I see that van again," he rallied on, "I promise I'm going to break a window!"

It was a rental anyway. I cast my hands in the air and walked out of the store, forgetting to search for Wendy's face as I left. I slipped onto the street where people were still picking apart our piles of memories. There was barely anything left. They had cleaned away our history like a plate of food, leaving nothing for latecomers. I tried to smile but it was a tough day. Moving puts its claws into us. It makes us watch as we tear up the foundations we've laid down. A room now sat empty where, full of aspirations, we had plugged in our amplifiers and faced each other with our instruments as the windows behind us looked out to the seemingly endless expanse of avenues, up past the Castro to the mysterious fog of Twin Peaks. That Church Street apartment had been a good home but perhaps we had stayed too long, pushed at the future of a band that we knew couldn't last. Perhaps the bed bugs had been sent to announce our resignation. A few weeks later a friend told me she'd seen the "For Rent" sign in our old window and when she said it I knew then that the old place was dead to me.

I liked the air of my new neighborhood. Although much quieter, the bustle of cars and people still permeated around the corners of my block and somehow that residual energy seeped into my skin. I have always needed a little bit of noise to stay alive. My roommates were kind but we were not friends yet. I didn't know it then but it would be my last apartment in the city before moving to the Midwest.

I closed the door to my room and wrote for hours or played guitar. I was practicing chords and melodies that would connect with new musicians and collaborators. I was no longer living at the center of activity. It was a quieter apartment, not the clubhouse for interconnecting scenes of friends. Instead, I became a satellite, the older guy who shows up to parties and gatherings at other people's places. I walked the streets of the neighborhood, learning the corners and cafés like a child in the hallways of a new school.

I bumped into Wendy one day. It was raining, only lightly, and we stood on the sidewalk, talking. We talked of shows that were coming up, which ones we'd go to and which ones we'd miss. A briefly awkward silence lingered between us. She mentioned her co-worker who had screamed at me and remarked that he hadn't been on his meds that day. We laughed—not cruelly but as a means to release a tension we had both quietly been holding. We said we looked forward to seeing each other again but we didn't make plans or exchange numbers. Instead we sulked back into the ether, into the moving parts of the system that sent us to work and beckoned us home. As I walked away from her, the sun began to push itself past the clouds. I heard the whirring of cars heaving up Duboce Avenue—the city, a machine in perennial churn. I would never see Wendy's face again. She faded like a final dispatch from an old life. I cut south across Guerrero, off to run an errand in the heart of the Mission. Indeed I had felt the warm charge in my chest that I had always felt for her. I had thought of asking her out and making concrete plans, getting a phone number and a date, but in the end it somehow seemed right just to let it go.

Heartland

Some Kinds of Love
(Are Better than Others)

A revolution in sexual celluloid.

Behind the Green Door, Marilyn Chambers' breakthrough skin flick was released in 1972. The film climaxed with a then unprecedented interracial sex scene between the white Chambers and the black Johnnie Keyes. It was a box-office hit.

Marilyn Chambers: When Johnnie put it in—it hurt. I had tears in my eyes. It just clicked. I went from being scared to "Yeah!" You can see it in my eyes. It was a primitive, animalistic type of thing. And then we were on our way.

Johnnie Keyes: I was acting like ten thousand Africans making up for that slavery shit. That's what I used as incentive to fuck Marilyn Chambers. I made love to Marilyn for about an hour and forty-three minutes without stopping… and then she fainted on me.[1]

*

Standing at the bar, the town's designated rock 'n' roll joint, he lays out his expectations for the night: drink a couple of beers, do a little bit of dancing, say hello to some friends and, ultimately, impress the new woman on his mind. He's been thinking about Monica for some time and she has returned his friendly glances.

---

1   Quotes taken from Legs McNeil and Jennifer Osborne's book, *The Other Hollywood: The Uncensored Oral History of the Porn Film Industry* (2006).

Reserved yet stylish, her hair is cut short, stopping halfway down her neck. Her eyes are fixed in a natural and attractive squint, inquisitive and inviting. He believes he likes her, has considered every detail of her Myspace[2] page and has come to the conclusion that her beauty resonates from all angles, no matter how hard the camera attempts to catch her off guard. Although he has sworn off cigarettes, he finds himself drawn to tobacco—to look cool—because she smokes as well. He puffs away liberally, the first pack he's bought since summer, and orders another beer as the buzz warms its arms around his shoulders.

He is 29 and he is a graduate student, a walking postponement of life's demands. Poor in pocket, rich in mind, he is an idealist and a dreamer. More specifically he is a writer, an essayist. In his particular program of study he is the only black male. Sometimes when he writes, his colleagues and professors wonder, in no intentionally malicious way, why the essay is not a black one, for indeed, if you talked of *this* or talked of *that*, it could be a black essay.

Most of them are quite nice, intelligent, and caring. So when he hears the expectations of his blackness called into question, he feels somewhat like a nigger unable to point to a single racist in the room. It certainly makes him feel alone in this place—the Midwest—with so few like himself.

But it's never just black. He feels alone in other ways too. The music he listens to and the clothes he wears—the tight jeans and retro t-shirts of the alternative generation—clash with his hypocritical disgust of the modern hipster's ironic poses. His embrace of liberal politics sits uneasily with his disdain for the Democratic Party. Likes the Grateful Dead, hates hippies. Curses corporate friends and their capitalist ways, yet enjoys drinking top-shelf bourbon and rubbing shoulders with

---

2   Myspace was a social media platform that achieved high popularity in the early to mid 2000s before being eclipsed by Facebook.

Southern gentlemen. Sometimes he's still trying to discover what it is he actually likes, what he might potentially love. He smiles on cue to please others while his mind quietly searches for a place to call home. He has considered that even if he were white he would be different and on his own. A romantic conceit perhaps, yet essentially wrong. If he were white he would have entrée to a club that often lets him in as a guest—after all, he went to the right schools and knows how to dance in the proper circles—but never as a member.

Inside he asks for simple human things such as to be loved or to have someone to come home to—someone who draws him in with how her skin grips the body, how her body reflects the soul and how her soul supports the being. His hue thickens: he becomes black *and* lonely, looking for love like everyone else. Everyone, at some point, must be a little bit black and a little bit lonely.

*

His brother's skin, like light-brown late-fall leaves, curved into the ice-queen's arms. It was the girl he had brought home from college. A Massachusetts girl. Blond hair and a blue gaze. She became a wife and those little ones became son and daughter. Nuclear, they retreated to their Boston home, charming kids by their sides, smiling.

If his parents have ever been unhappy about his brother's interracial union, they've never said a thing about it. The graduate wonders, *Whom can I bring home to the parents?*—considers that two white women might be too many in a family with only two black sons. His mother would show the sets of wedding pictures to her friends. *Oh honey*, they would say, *where'd you go wrong with these handsome boys? They sure got the fever, don't they? Civil rites, sugar. You get what you ask for.*

At home, before the bar, he moved past the pictures and read the "About Me" section on Monica's Myspace page. He learned that she is: *habitually late, broke, forgetful, stressed out, and lucky. She is stuck in this mid-western town for an indeterminate amount of time, in limbo, between a failed attempt at attending a private women's college in Massachusetts and whatever comes next. She sells expensive clothing and greeting cards to pay the rent, and has found a consumeristic place in her heart that actually doesn't mind working retail. When business is slow, daydreams an idealistic future in which she lives in a booming metropolis, has an MFA, and frequently throws big, splashy parties.*

"I'm going to New York in November," Monica says to him at the bar.

He considers her white skin, noticing how something so pale can also be so rich. He shifts in a little closer, wanting to kiss the beauty mole on her left cheek but knowing he can't do it, not just yet. "Oh cool, for what?"

"Just to wander around the streets aimlessly."

"Forever?"

"No, just vacation."

"You know, I've got this guide to New York I typed up for a friend. Well, not really New York. More like Manhattan. Because I don't know shit about Brooklyn. Actually, not true, I've been to Brooklyn a bunch—the Brooklyn Museum is mint—but just don't know enough to type up a Brooklyn list. But I've got the Manhattan list. Totally biased to the Lower East Side. Hipster cliché, I know. But it's cool down there. How 'bout I email it to you?"

She smiles at him. "That would be nice but I really do like to wander around and get lost."

"Maybe just print it out and put it in your back pocket?"

Her smile widens a bit and he catches a glimpse of her teeth. He thinks of a tongue wrapped around his own and a warm body in his bed; they are walking together, hands interlocked, on the streets of their small town. He decides then and there that he definitely likes her. His beer emptied, he takes off for the dance floor. Riding the alcohol, the tobacco, and the high of romantic possibility, he moves to the sounds. He has always wanted to be moved.

The guitar hooks are vicious and he can thrash like a white punk. It's a Bloc Party song and it makes him lose his mind. The riff is dangerous, the drums are electrical charges, and the singer is black. He wipes the sweat from his brow and sees Ellen, a fellow writer, on the dance floor. They hug briefly. Her skin is brown like his and she is first generation, her parents South Asian immigrants to the States. She's not quite black, he thinks, but certainly not white. They share a language—the language of Diaspora—and hold a common understanding beneath the surface of their barroom banter. On late nights they sit on his apartment floor—the low hum of beats pulsing in the background—and talk with an openness not afforded to them in more public social venues. He looks at her in the bar and she smiles—*it's great to see you here*—takes his cigarette and dances away to a far corner of the floor.

He notices another girl on the dance floor—kind of knows her but doesn't really *know* her: in shoebox towns one collects familiar faces like bottle caps. Her name is Connie. She is small, cute, and loud: a firecracker with freckles. Recognizing him, she smiles and grabs his hand. "Let's dance," she says.

She looks him in the eyes, the music loud. "I love black cock," she shouts.

She turns around laughing to a friend and returns her eyes to his, affirming their collective ethos.

"We *love* black cock. Come dance."

Pornographers conjure up scripts in valley towns outside of Los Angeles. A new script seems to write itself. Not just one script but an entire inevitable genre of pornography. It fulfills our projected fantasies of eager white girls in love with massive black appendages. She will kneel before the camera. Looking into it, she'll tell us, *Yeah, I want that big black cock. Where is it and how long do I have to wait for it?* The director, likely a white man, will orchestrate this piece of modern erotic cinema. A black man will enter the frame, excited for showtime. She offers a blow-job, but no, a vicious skull-fucking, which looks more like a gaffing than an act of love, will be impressed upon her mouth, throat, neck. An anal will occur. Perhaps, a double-penetration, the gaping of what was once whole.

The picture will fortify certain stereotypes: black guys have huge penises. White women wanna get stuck ruefully by the homeboys. Dark-skinned men secretly plot to carve out fair-skinned women behind the suspecting backs of white men and black women—and when they do they will collapse the white women like lions pounce their prey.

The Pornographer as Artist tells us the scenes are beautiful; they arouse everyone on the set and all of us at home, in dark American bedrooms, our fiber-optic cables sweating under the weight of the stream. The Pornographer as Businessman remarks that he shoots the films because people will pay for them. After all, he is not just in this for the art. He must manufacture the products that people want to buy.

Capitalism and culture rent rooms in the same flat and they get along just fine, sharing ideas, an interdisciplinary relationship. The low-income renters downstairs can't stand the noise. Yet we all tune in. We acknowledge that the villain of the story is not always villainous but rather embodies "the intriguing" or "a desire" or "a question demanding an answer."

*

On the dance floor in the bar, the firecracker, Connie, had posed a question disguised as a comment—an inquiry he didn't want to answer. An invitation: you will come dance with us, no? Your black cock hanging, swinging to a beat. *It was more than a joke*, he thinks. From one perspective, one that leaves the trauma of American history aside, it is such a pleasant offer: *I'll sleep with you because your skin is beautiful*. At once he feels so desired and yet so different, the prized other. He can't believe Connie said those words. It was like something he'd expect to hear in a dirty teen-movie or a skit on a rap album. From a close friend it would have been a joke, a risqué tug at the comfort zone's edges. Coming from someone he hardly knows, he doesn't know what to make of it but he can already feel a desire burning inside, the desire to fuck, not to love, but to fuck Connie, because she, on one level or another, seriously or humorously, or both, has let him know what she'd like to have in her bed. And yet another condition to add to his expanding list: blackness, loneliness, and now the charged, perhaps uncontrollable urge to play into the role of the desired other.

He returns to Monica and finds her quiet and smiling: a hometown girl and someone to hold on to.

"This is a good night," she says.

"Yeah, totally," he replies.

Around them, the bar relaxes into closing time. Everyone is smiles and loud speech, as if the night has just begun. Groups form, dissolve, and reform. Monica speaks of an after-hours. He watches as Connie and Monica lock arms, deduces that they are friends. Connie collapses into Monica's group and heads to the party. Her words continue to startle him and to steadily engage his crotch. Ellen, his friend with skin like his, walks by, poking him on the shoulder. "Hey, playa, you going to the after-party?"

"Yeah, I think so."

"Good choice, sir, good choice."

They step into the late-evening air. "It's cold as fuck out here," someone says.

Indeed, it's the first chill of the season.

*

He watches the various characters from a distance and laughs. There goes Mande after Mark again. There goes Mark dodging Mande's attempts, singing beer songs with Mike. And there is Sergei, confused, with a beer in hand, not quite sure whom to go after. The graduate slouches in chairs, wondering how time will turn. The alcohol props up his back, tugs at his trousers. Yet another night stretched long. *And why*, he asks, searching in earnest for what makes him give up sleep and clear mornings. For love? Is it a youthful energy that he's not ready to give up? There's something about those hours from 2 a.m. to 6 a.m.: the nether-hours. They become an ocean of unreachable desires. Every now and then you shore upon islands of answers. The morning, though, reveals them as sirens.

He is in a basement apartment for the after-party. It belongs to one of Monica's friends. He thinks of Monica and a move he should make. In the kitchen, he sees Connie again, now with her arms around Ellen. Another surprising friendship, he reckons. Connie approaches him and whispers in his ear.

"Monica likes you."

"Yeah."

"She's a wonderful kisser and *I* should know: we're roommates."

"Well that's cool. She's great."

"You should go for it."

"I think I will."

He walks into the living room, considers for a moment that all of the people might really be listening to Men at Work. There is a makeshift bedroom in one of the far corners, separated from everything else by a curtain of sheets. A familiar voice calls for him from the bedroom. It's Monica, lying in her friend's bed, as if it's her own, with a few other young women, eating pizza and goofing off. With her beckoning hand, she gestures for him to join. He slides under the covers and grabs a slice of pizza. As they lean into each other, he can feel the skin on her neck, then her cheek on his.

"You're warm," she says.

The party is a hum. A few remain in the kitchen, talking through the motions: late-night slugs sliding about, sipping the ends of beer cans, contemplating sleep. He is in bed, fully clothed with a cigarette and a beer, next to Monica. Their legs mix and his hand runs through her hair. They kiss, the good kiss Connie told him about. *This could be something*, he thinks, *someone to hold on to*. Maybe a girl to bring home. He wonders, *Is it crazy to think this after only one kiss?* He bends down and speaks softly, "I'll see you tomorrow, okay?" Another kiss and Monica's eyes drift away like two old stars about to turn off.

Outside, the chill encases his ears. Different flocks of the broken-winged spread out across the street, scattering in directions east, north, south, and west to dark homes and empty beds. He had hoped that Connie would be gone by now, but there she is, in front of him, her arms wrapped around Ellen, both of their eyes looking to him for guidance. *Poor leader you've chosen*, he thinks.

"I can drive you ladies home," he offers.

"Are you sure you can drive?" Ellen asks him.

"Maybe."

"Really?"

"Yeah, sure. I got it."

He turns to Connie. "Where do you live?"

She lives too far away. Ellen sighs, looking sad and fatigued. Her eyes talk to him and he understands that she wants to go to sleep immediately.

"You guys can crash at my place."

"Are you sure? Is that cool?"

"You two take the bed and I'll take the couch. I'll drive you home in the morning."

"You're such a gentleman."

His nerves unravel. He can see the embers glowing in Connie's eyes and while he wishes he could teleport away, he knows he must tend to the infant flames. Like a film actor out of body, he watches himself walk through scenes yet to be shot. Turn left here, the feet up the steel stairs he knows so well, down a hallway, a key in a door, opening up to a room and a scene. *Welcome to my place. Sorry for the mess.*

He brushes his teeth and it is like slow motion, his ears ringing in the silence of the bathroom, bruises from the loud songs in the bar. He walks across his living room and makes his way for the couch only to find it taken. Ellen is a ball, curled up with a blanket. She looks up at him. "No, no, honey, you take your bed."

He responds, an anxiety in his voice. "I don't think you understand. You should sleep in there with Connie."

"No, no," she says. "It's all you."

Ellen rolls over, smiling and bringing the blanket to her chin as if she's done him a favor.

Connie sits on the edge of his bed. They touch hands and then fuck hard. Monica is a past tense.

*

Driving her home in the morning he notices that the day isn't as cold as the night had suggested. If Connie had wanted him, he argues quietly in his head, in the way Monica had wanted him—not for the novelty of black sexuality but for the entire mixed package, it would have been different. He feels stained for giving in and as he pushes the car forward across a large intersection, he thinks of how Monica will label him "asshole" and, even worse, "sketchy," in the overlapping social circles of their small community. He cringes. Nothing worse than someone calling you asshole and having to acknowledge they're right.

He also can't deny that Connie's proposition and his passionate concurrence was thoroughly intriguing and satisfying, something he longed for as much as he despised himself for failing to refuse it. Her timing had jammed his gears. How stained would he actually feel had Connie enticed him a few days earlier, before he had connected with Monica? Maybe the event would have become a funny story to share at the bar with the guys. It also seems as if it would have been easier to leave Connie to her own devices had she not infused his skin into her advances, if he hadn't been asked to play his title role in this Midwestern town: the role of the "other."

He pulls up to her driveway and puts an index finger to Connie's lips as if to *ssshhh* her. "Not a word to Monica," he tells her. She smirks as if he told a joke, as if he really thinks there is any chance of covering this up. "Yes, not a word. See you around." A little secret everyone knows in a small town. First worms, then dawn's crows.

*

Interviewer: Are you a painter or a *black* painter?

> **Artist (Basquiat):** Oh I use a lot of colors, not just black...

Interviewer: Do you feel you're being exploited or are you yourself exploiting the white image of the black artist from the ghetto?

Artist (Basquiat): Are those the only two possibilities?[3]

---

3   Quoted from Julian Schnabel's original screenplay for the film *Basquiat* (1996).

Some of Us Are Very Hungry Now

1

Miranda had driven me three and a half hours from Iowa City
to O'Hare so that I could catch my plane to Hong Kong and
I wasn't sure if I loved her anymore. We were cracking like old
paint but we weren't old, we were young. She knew she would
leave in the fall and I knew that our kind of love was not the
kind to be tested by distance, which is to suggest that it wasn't
love at all. I wanted to pull away without hurting her. She was
moving to a rural town in the Rust Belt to work in the library of
a distinguished liberal arts college. Iowa City was like a metropolis compared to that tiny town. We never wanted to admit it but
we knew she would be lonely there. We knew she would need
me and I didn't want to be needed. But I needed that ride to the
airport and I needed someone to pick me up when I returned
a month later so I played the whole thing with a straight face.
With these thoughts of romantic desolation and the inevitable,
encroaching dissolution of a relationship that had been brief
but passionate, I kissed her goodbye and checked in for the long
flight across the world.

I am not sure why I even went to Hong Kong. I think it was
simply because I could go. And because I *could* I knew that
I *should*. I was in a writing program at the University of Iowa
and our director had arranged a study abroad opportunity, most
of which was paid for by the university. I was also on staff at
an online music magazine. I wrote features and reviewed new
album releases. My editor had been talking to me about Hong
Kong. He thought I should write a piece about the underground

music scene. The magazine was perpetually interested in uncovering new sounds and cultures. He told me I could write *the* piece about the Hong Kong scene. It was an opportunity, he said, that I couldn't turn down.

In some ways, he was correct. It was Hong Kong. It was another part of the world. How could I not go? Iowa City, while layered with more complexity than most people would expect, was beginning to feel small. I had been there two years since moving from San Francisco and I missed the anonymity of the bigger city: the rush of walking down avenues where no one had seen me before, of sitting in bars where they didn't care where I was from as long as I bought drinks, of meeting jagged, worn humans whose missing pieces fit in with my own fractured puzzle, of loving them once and waking up in a neighborhood I had never experienced—running out of the door before they returned from the bathroom, back onto the street where no one gave two shits about my wrinkled shirts and broken values. I need to feel alone and I need buildings to look at. I need to lose my sightlines within the masses of people whose passions are not my own.

I had first met Miranda at a party at the Writers' House. She rolled her eyes and said, "So what kind of music are you into?" She had said it in a way that it was clear she would disagree with me no matter what came out of my mouth. I was afraid and aroused. We sat on a couch and the party boomed around us, people pushing liquor down their throats. They called it the Writers' House because poets and novelists lived there and they drank and procrastinated, sometimes they wrote. The university paid their rent. Miranda's hair was short and blond. She wore dark glasses in sturdy plastic frames. "What do you think about Animal Collective?" she asked.

"They're okay, I guess."

"Oh god," she said and those eyes rolled again. "You don't even understand them."

We argued for several minutes and when she stood up I noticed how tall she was. She peered at me through her glasses as we went on about music. A friend beckoned me from across the room. "I am sorry," I said. "I have to go. I hope to see you around."

"Yeah," she said. "I guess so." She put up a wall of disinterest when she said it but I sensed just behind that façade an element of curiosity, the first spark that might bring us together.

I saw her the next day in a coffee shop. She wore snug jeans and had a sack of books under her arm. She comported herself with the style of an artist and the posture of an academic. Her eyes were small, round, and distinct. Her gaze was sharp.

"It is really great to see you," I said.

"Yes," she said. "It's good to see you too."

She smiled for the first time and something in me—beyond my control, beyond my logic—opened up. Just then, I decided my approach would be glacial: no drunken one-nighters and awkward hung-over brunches. I would approach her with class. I would lay my sport coat upon murky puddles and she would trot across, her nose and her eyes pointing up toward the sky. A healthy conversation led to a respectful date which led to a faint kiss and another date led us to bed and after yet another date we concluded that we would be together for a very long time. I told her my secrets—embarrassments that I couldn't bear anyone else to know and she was okay with them. That lifted the weight of a thousand stones from my soul. Then she told me her secrets and I was okay with her secrets but she wasn't. She was tormented by them. And I sat in her bed, staring at her back and then staring at the wall and it was then that I knew we all had secrets and scars that we carried around. Like an otherworldly flash I suddenly understood that a lover is there to touch those scars and massage them— not to make you forget them but to help heal them. It was an opportunity—and also a burden—that I hadn't entirely deduced until then.

2

The buildings on Hong Kong Island, from the offices down-town to the residential haunts, were looming giants. It was a land of business. Commerce unfolded around me like a national pas-time. The downtown financial district was simply called Central. Efficiency was key. A dim sum restaurant in Central could very well be named Central Dim Sum Restaurant #9. I was looking at an apartment building with a friend and we were counting the units by estimation, trying to figure out how many people lived in it. 10,000? 20,000? Four of those buildings might comprise the entire population of Iowa City—they reached up, long phal-lic intrusions pointing toward the tropical sky. People were fluid, the lifeblood thriving through the streets. Our group stayed in a special visitors' residence hall at the University of Hong Kong, up in the hills tucked away from Central. I ascended a series of escalators that carried me from Central up a massive incline into an area called the Mid-Levels. The journey stretched for 15 minutes, by far the most time I had ever spent on escalators at one time.

I made an assumption: A city like Hong Kong, with its robust capitalism, would also have an artistic underground, a creative antithesis to the corporate structure around it. So many cities—Amsterdam, London, New York—seemed to exist like this: pockets of creativity flowing with and against the financial mar-kets around them. Hong Kong wore its own complex cloth—a city stitched between the economic identities of the West and mainland China. I conjured up a daydream, a landscape filled with thousands of Hong Kongers clutching their guitars and coughing out a sonic revolution at the buildings, the escalators, and the money. I believed there were bands that would change me, emitting sounds from instruments and songbooks I'd never heard. Every place cultivates a scene.

The popular sound in Hong Kong was Cantopop—American-style pop songs sung in the local dialect, Cantonese. Some of them were pop songs you had heard before. A number of Cantopop artists lifted melodies and chord progressions from classic as well as contemporary Western, Korean, and Japanese songs and overlaid their own Cantonese lyrics on top of these familiar tunes. Imagine Stevie Wonder's "I Just Called to Say I Love You" in a different language with a new meaning. In the popular bars, the Cantopop bands might go as far as playing full cover sets to satisfy expats and Western pop admirers. The concept was lucrative if not entirely original.

I established contact with an arts reporter at *Hong Kong Magazine* named Spike. We never met face to face, but corresponded by email while I sat in computer labs at the university or in coffee shops near Central. Spike explained that the global music labels relied on Cantopop to drive revenue with its easily digestible, image-based pop. It was a faithful machine that could produce regional stars.

Cantopop thrived in the expensive expat bars of the Lan Kwai Fong neighborhood, where happy hours ran from 4 p.m. until midnight. Drinking in Lan Kwai Fong was like drinking in Times Square or Fisherman's Wharf. The cover bands took the stage at tourist traps, wrapping airtight versions of everything from The Supremes to Sublime around the ears of cheery, rosy-faced expats, mostly businessmen from the U.K., mainland EU, and Australia. I recalled the cover bands back in the States with names that fully revealed their programmatic conceits: Tainted Love, AC/DShe. You wanted a product, you wanted a memory—your '70s disco indulgences, your misguided '80s materialism, your Gen-X '90s slackerism—and it was reproduced for you, for a price, for fun, for the betterment of your condition on a Saturday night in the city after a week in the office, a reprieve from that slowly descending machine under which you were caught, under which you would eventually be crushed.

I went to a Cantopop bar in Lan Kwai Fong. I ushered past the initial gang of tourist energy swelling around the bar—white faces happy to see other white faces after a long day of venturing on foreign streets. My dark skin punctuated all scenes in this town—on the streets, in the local eateries, and in the tourist bars. When I encountered another black person they were often from a country in Africa. I was happy to see them—distant cousins—navigating a different but not unfamiliar set of hurdles to the ones I faced at home.

I strolled to the back area of the bar and looked up at the stage. A full band raged on—guitar, bass, drums, keyboards, and a female singer. I couldn't believe it—they were so tight. They didn't miss a note. The grooves had been entirely duplicated from a history of pop music. I looked at them, embarrassed to be there and amazed that they had infused so much effort and skill into performing a replica. White businessmen danced around me—fellows in their suits, ties loosened, their eyes sunken into their skulls. Around the edges of the fray there stood the older white businesswomen, no longer optimistic, just tired. Some job, some opportunity had pulled all of them into the orbit of Hong Kong and now that they had been here for so long it seemed impossible to move back home. They wasted away their nights into their 30s and 40s in bars with music copied and pasted from someone else's canon. They were more interested in familiarity than discovery. Inside I scoffed at them and their dreamless auras. In their failures to find passion elsewhere, they found respite in the predictable thrall of a Cantopop bar for expats. They made their rounds—and they too had been rounded out by others—through the other expats their age, eventually finding some new tourist or expatriate meat, pulverized by a succession of beers and shots. I winced at the thought of being drawn into such a trap. I would stay pure among these wolves.

I retreated from the bar, sober and hungry, to my quarters at the university. I took a bus that escalated from the heart of the city—past a Kentucky Fried Chicken packed with locals—and into the relative calm of the hills.

3

"In college," Miranda said, "I was a hipster. I was one of the cool kids." She meant, I think, to impart on me that, despite my literary pursuits and vibrant interest in music, she hovered above me on a higher artistic plain. She had studied art and she had been a painter. I asked her, much to her annoyance and passive disdain, why she didn't paint anymore, why she pursued a degree in library science. "Just 'cause," she said repeatedly. "You have to live, right?"

Miranda took me to a show at a place called the Hall Mall in Iowa City. Her friends played in a band called Raccoo-oo-oon. The Hall Mall was just a dusty hallway on the second floor of a building that housed a few makeshift endeavors—a tattoo shop, a place that sold used DVDs and VHS tapes, and a couple of rooms rented out by bands for practice space. Young punks, post-punks, and aging punks crowded the slim hallway, their bodies slowly tilting back and forth in tandem with the currents of psychedelic static emanating from Raccoo-oo-oon, who played not on a stage but in the middle of the floor. There were perhaps one or two loose fixtures hanging from the ceiling— long batches of cords ending in naked, harsh light bulbs that swung above our heads. The musicians concocted a pleasurable racket. The vocals were tertiary—they settled in, via waves of delay, behind furious tom rolls and an absolute wall of guitar noise. This music was something to be *felt* not simply *regarded* from a distance. Perhaps it had been intended as a blunt reaction to the long tradition of folk-blues and Americana that had anchored itself in the black Iowa dirt. Or perhaps it was just a bunch of art school kids who wanted to emote, who wanted to shout rather than whisper, because they were angry and frustrated but not quite sure why.

After the show, Miranda talked to her friends in the band. The guitarist, Shawn, was the king of the pack—not just the band, but the entire energetic posse that swelled around them, all kids in their asymmetric glory with tight jeans (one leg torn off) and unorthodox haircuts (one side long, the other shaved short). When Shawn looked at me, he conveyed with his eyes, likely unintentionally, that I was something different from him, different from his people. When he spoke to me—"Hey, man, how's everything?"—he kind of looked away from me as if there was someone else he would rather speak to but he still had enough manners to engage on a surface level. I think he was wearing a multi-colored tank top awash in sweat. Either through his intense disaffection with me or my bubbling insecurity it became clear that he was underground and I was normal. I was just a writer. We writers wore battered, worn-in oxfords and patched-up sweaters and drank La Crosse Light, PBR, and Jim Beam at the Fox Head on the north side of town. We were predictable creatures who touched down in Iowa City for two or three years before rewinding to New York, San Francisco, or whichever coastal town we had left our hearts in. Or maybe Shawn just thought I was some guy he didn't know who was dating an old friend of his, who having left the circle of underground art, was perhaps someone he didn't feel like he knew that well anymore. Miranda, I think, sensed my discomfort. It hung around me like an apparition.

"Let's go," she said. We walked away from the Hall Mall. I felt a bit displaced though thoroughly intrigued as if I had seen some piece of Iowa City that had been hidden from me all along—the suggestion, no, the existence of a *scene*, of a life force that pulsed beneath the commonplace patterns of the community into which it was placed.

I talked to Miranda and other friends to learn more about Shawn. He ran a cassette and record label out of his house called Night-People Records. He literally made cassettes in his room on a dubbing system with a master tape running the music out to several copies at once. Then he packaged the tapes with art he had designed himself. The vinyl had to be produced at a plant but when the records came back he made the art for those as well. His operation shipped music all over the world. He specialized in various strands of psych music, bands whose sounds were sepia and day-glo at once, analog and antique and layered and electronic. Shawn's music was technically underground; it didn't even register a blip in the world of people who downloaded mainstream country, pop, or rap music. But when he toured, there existed a network of people like him—people who had made their own systems underneath the populist apparatus of music distribution—and he could play shows with those people and their fans in Baltimore, Oakland, Brooklyn, any community, really, across the country and even the world. Most people in Iowa City—the lawyers, doctors, city workers—didn't know him, but he could travel thousands of miles and there were people there who knew his label and had heard his music. He was part of a small scene stretched across hundreds of little intersections on a world map. Occasionally one of the bands from the interconnected family of scenes would pop its head ever so slightly into popular culture, acts like No Age, Peaking Lights, or Zola Jesus who had spent years playing DIY house shows. All of a sudden they'd be doing a special project at the Getty or MoMA. The gatekeepers would anoint their projects as "high art" and deem it appropriate for the readers of the *New Yorker*. I met a poet from Brooklyn who had come to pursue his MFA at Iowa. I asked him why he had come here and he said, "Well the program obviously. And Night-People Records. I would like to meet Shawn." He said it like there was mystique around it. Really, it was just the one guy—tall, smart, and determined, who had made this aesthetic, this idea in a basement in a house tucked away in the rustic pastiche of downtown Iowa City.

I was rethinking my stance on Animal Collective. They had not just created music, they had created a world. The songs didn't always move within the familiar narratives of beginnings and endings; rather they morphed in and out of different emotional states of mind. The voices came from an odd cohort—Panda Bear, Avey Tare, Geologist, Deakin—and the sounds seemed to have been pulled from warped, invented instruments. There was something vaguely primal about their songs—the insistent *thwap* of mutant tom drums, the vocal chants, and the avant-garde freak-outs, all of this surrounded by a fog of effected guitars and synths and field recording samples. The band's members, a group of old friends, had migrated between Baltimore and Brooklyn as they developed their sound. Their albums might feature all of the members or just some of them—whoever was around at the time of the writing and recording. As members floated in and out of the collective, the band's textural vibe continued to evolve. It was like a collaborative painting with one artist adding a few strokes one afternoon and two others coming in to work on the canvas for the rest of the week. At once they were hippies, punks, and dedicated artistes. Avey Tare wrote the first album during college in New York. What began as extremely abstract musings slowly became weird yet catchy compositions. Within those songs the masses might recognize unmistakable hints of both early psych and the odd visions of songwriters like Syd Barrett and Brian Wilson. Pockets of underground scenes evolved around Animal Collective's ethos—it is important to state that while a lot of bands were directly influenced by their sound there are as many that seemed to be influenced by the idea of them: free-living musicians making music the way they wanted that was neither wildly popular nor resolutely inapproachable. I saw in Shawn and his Night-People community a similar attitude, the notion that you can build your own scene, your own world and thus connect with the networks of other worlds across the globe who might not sound like you but think like you.

4

I read about a show at a club called The Wanch, part of an ongoing series named Plug + Play. I took the MTR to the Wan Chai District. The heat outside the subway was gripping; it hung around me as I stepped into the crowded, overrun avenue. The street lights burned a little darker in Wan Chai. There was commerce and wealth but less flash. It felt a little hungrier on those streets, less tourist-friendly, more for the locals who knew their way around.

I found The Wanch on a quieter avenue, tucked away from the hum of main-street action. It was an intimate pub: small, cozy, and simple. The bar opened to a performance space in one corner. No stage, just bands on the floor. I saw quite a few white people mixed in with the local Hong Kongers. Whites in Hong Kong mostly seemed like garnish dropped on top of a dish as a finishing touch. Interesting, I had thought, to have the white people marginalized. Though in The Wanch, there was still a solid contingent, enough to have a presence. I didn't see any other black people, so, in more than one way, I was there alone.

I stood at the bar, sipping a beer, measuring the time until the band started. A web of voices courted my attention—a mix of English, Aussie, and Kiwi accents as well as Cantonese, and even the Hong Kongers who spoke in English. I also heard a couple of American girls. They were louder, I thought, than everyone else—or perhaps I was drawn to their voices, looking for some element of connection. They wore tight dark jeans and slim-fitting tops cutting sharply into the contours of their slight figures. I thought briefly about talking to them, about introducing myself as a tourist from back home, as a music writer looking to know more about the scene, but I felt embarrassed not only by the prospect of talking to people I did not know but at the possibility of them turning down my company, further alienating me from everyone and everything else in The Wanch before the band had even plugged in. I would rather be alone than exposed.

The Sinister Left finally began. The band was loud and the bar was rather small. They imparted a crass reduction of British influences—the psychedelic gloom of Black Rebel Motorcycle Club (an American-born, U.K.-influenced band—*already* once removed from the source material) and the arena-sized melodrama of Radiohead. The effect was that we, the audience, heard something familiar but that we also didn't hear anything new or essential. I held my ground. This was the first true rock band I had seen in Hong Kong. They didn't have to be perfect. Discovery was never immediate. It took patience and persistence.

The crowd hovered in the small area in front of the band, faithfully transfixed. A new group, The Lovesong elicited fury: punk rock with slippery time changes and start-stop explosions. I followed their movements, the feverish jerks of forearms and elbows across the bodies of guitars. The beer rushed to my senses and I felt myself attracted to the sweaty pulp of the crowd. The American girls danced aggressively. For a moment the signals of music from my youth—Fugazi, Jawbox—attuned me to the ethos of The Lovesong. By the time the final band, Elf Fatima, started their set, my emotions had become pliable. I relaxed into their wash of post-rock brooding—studious valleys and loud, crushing peaks.

At the bar, awaiting a beer, I met an Australian named Paul who had been living in Hong Kong for 10 years. He told me that he just showed up one day and never left. "The local scene," he said, "is nonexistent. It's dismal." I laughed. Inside, I thought he was wrong, that he just hadn't tried hard enough. Though, his precise criticism shook me from my trance, from my comfortable lull into familiarity. I questioned everything I had just seen.

He projected a thick vibration of expatriate disaffection. He reminded me of the older townies in Iowa City, the ones who sunk in the bars in the late afternoon and didn't leave until the late evening. They sat there complaining—no good music, no good kids, no good nothing—and yet, even though they rejected the culture, they remained in town, fully settled, disinterested in the idea of finding something else. It wasn't the culture that brought them down but rather themselves. How long, I wondered, before that became me, before I became Paul.

I awoke with an opaque head. My muddled thoughts mirrored the humidity of the Hong Kong morning outside. I thought about writing but I was too tired to open my laptop. Instead, I jotted notes in my journal, trying to make sense of what I had experienced the previous evening. I had an ache that stretched from my temple back along the edge of my head. It seemed to stop around my left ear. The pain loitered persistently, not unbearable but disturbing. I needed water and ibuprofen. As I sobered up, the critical voice of my editor haunted me from thousands of miles away. With my back propped against the wall and the sheets pulled up to my waist, I revisited my experience at The Wanch. I asked myself if anything I had seen the night before had rivaled anything I could see back home. I kept turning it over and coming back with the same answer: no. I had not encountered revelation; instead I had lazily wallowed in comfort. I had found nothing new and therefore my empty article had little to ground itself on as a shepherd of discovery. I resolved or perhaps hoped that the bands I had seen at The Wanch were just one element of what was surely a diverse scene. There were other bands—yes—there were others out there in Hong Kong, unveiling brilliant sounds from the basement.

I took a bus downtown from the heights of the University of Hong Kong campus. I set up my laptop in a café and emailed with Spike from *Hong Kong Magazine*. I told him that I had seen some decent bands but nothing particularly new.

How many bands out there worked within a vacuum? What was the actual capacity for new music, for new art?

I took more ibuprofen, I drank more coffee, and I drank more beer yet the pain in my head at the edge of my ear pulsed doggedly beneath the surface.

5

I hovered above Miranda, our naked bodies pushing back and forth. Her face contorted. Her teeth clenched. Her eyes closed. She looked unhappy. Her expression recalled someone working out in the gym, lifting that one last rep or running that final mile on the treadmill. Sex as necessity, as self-improvement, as pain in exchange for being a better, healthier person. Not as enjoyment, not as love but as duty. I wondered what my face looked like. Did I have a pleasant face? A sad face? Or was I stoic, emotionless, and Spartan? I couldn't make her happy in bed. It takes time, she once told me. I couldn't break past the seal that separated our most intimate elements. We were close but not together.

Her apartment didn't offer much room—a small kitchen, low ceilings, a cramped bedroom, and a single bathroom. We looked like misplaced giants in her place, both of us over six feet tall. Miranda had some of her paintings in the corner of her bedroom. She seemed to ignore them, to deny their existence. They were brilliant works. We were dressed and now she was cooking on the stove, something easy, something simple. I was leaning in the doorjamb between the bedroom and the kitchen. I asked her, "Why did you stop making art?" She didn't look at me, she just kept cooking.

"I didn't stop forever. I am just taking a break." She kept turning her food over in the pan—green beans, tofu, or whatever it was. "I will start again. I don't know when."

She was on sabbatical, I suppose. It unnerved me. I couldn't understand why she wouldn't *make* art if she, someone who clearly beamed with talent, *could* make art. Her parents had offered to support her if she pursued an MFA—and they weren't rich—but still she had chosen an advanced degree in library science. "I needed to do something real," she told me. Library science could lead to a real job. Her sense of personal responsibility, at the expense of her passion, seemed so traditional to me, so textbook Iowan, as if her people had just descended last week from the Old World into the plains of America, looking for opportunities, for a safe, new life. I respected it. She possessed a common sense I had yet to exhibit.

"Any more questions?" she asked, looking at me now.

"No," I said. "No."

I eased from the doorway and lay down on her bed. I certainly didn't hold the same sense of responsibility that she did. I was wasteful with my time at best. On good days, when I didn't have class, I woke up, remained in bed for a few hours while reading. I would put on a record and look out my window. I would leave the apartment for 45 minutes to eat a cheap breakfast at the diner a block away. Then I would come home and write for two hours. Then I would write songs on the guitar. Then I would go to the bar a block away to work on revisions. I would write there, ordering a three-dollar cheeseburger and a 7UP for a buck—all this while people worked around me, punched nine-to-five cards at the factory, the office, the store, worked third shifts and crap jobs. Eventually I would have a beer and then the happy hour crowd would arrive. Beers turned into whiskeys with small beer backs behind them. I drank until late, ordering another three-dollar cheeseburger for dinner, and then went home where I slept, awaiting the pattern to repeat.

We had mandatory workshops at nine in the morning in Hong Kong. The workshops were a bureaucratic failure. They happened because the University of Iowa was paying for the trip and as such there needed to be some legitimate academic behavior, some indelible proof that we had actually learned something. And yet, the least amount of learning happened in that bare, rundown classroom where we discussed each other's work, both dehydrated physically and disinterested spiritually. The professors and the students jointly acknowledged that the learning, or in some cases the dismantling, happened on the streets, away from the visitors' dorms, computer labs, and class-rooms of the University of Hong Kong. Real learning would be catching a serious case of the clap and figuring out how to cure it without anyone else knowing, or getting punched out by Triad gangsters and locating a nice makeup store to help cover up the shiners. I had awoken for workshop one day and felt like my head was going to explode. My headache had become a tortur-ous earache. How could I listen to new music with an earache?

One of the creative writing students had shared a dense essay concerning a visit to ice-pits in southern France. There was a ripe intelligence to the literature but its disguise of clear nar-rative and fierce compactness of millions of ideas in each rich paragraph sent pangs across my ear, my face, my will. I survived workshop but asked for a pass on afternoon group activities. I needed a doctor. Someone from the university put me in a cab. They sent me, I think, to a former British hospital but I am not quite sure. The cab climbed a hill, taking me high into the upper regions of Hong Kong Island. I was dropped off at the hos-pital and checked into outpatient care. The hospital was quiet and clean. Everyone spoke English exceptionally. I felt safe, at home on this distant island. Although I had arrived without an appointment I only waited 20 minutes for care. A doctor saw me, a kind, middle-aged Chinese man. He took a close look at my ear and determined I had an infection. I had sensitive ears but to catch an infection: I felt like I was six years old. The kind doctor gave me a bottle of antibiotics. He said I would be fine in a few days. I asked when I could start drinking again. He said to take it easy. I checked out and paid for the whole experience with my credit card. It came to about 50 U.S. dollars. I took a cab back down the hill and thought about how the care had been so accessible and oddly affordable.

I retreated into the sights of Hong Kong, not forgetting the music scene, just putting it on hold. I went to a highly recommended dim sum restaurant. It was in a vast gray room on the second floor of a building on a busy street. The menu didn't have pictures, just a long list in Cantonese. I sat at a big round table, staring at the characters, figuring out which ones I would point to.

An old man, mostly bald except for some black and gray hairs curving around the sides and back of his head, sat down next to me. He nodded and I smiled at him politely. He motioned for the menu with his hand. That's all he did and I understood everything. I gave him the menu and he looked it over briefly before putting it down on the table. The waiter stopped by, looked at me, and saw that I was useless. He turned to the old man who clattered off a number of items. The waiter ran back to the kitchen. I looked at the man and we smiled at each other. I thanked him with that smile. He looked ahead at a far wall and we sat there awaiting our food in silence.

I took a tram to the top of Hong Kong Peak. One of the highest points on the island, its vista overlooked much of the city and beyond. I paid 10 dollars and rode the tram up the side of a mountain toward the peak, the ride almost frightening in its extreme vertical ascent. As I exited the tram, I found myself in a mall. In order to reach the vista I would need to scale five stories of escalators through a dizzying hall of commerce; all this to simply catch a view of the city. I paid another 10 bucks for access to the view.

The peak itself was sweltering. Tourists scurried about its edges, snapping pictures and sweating. The view astounded from all points. We looked down on the city and its thick congealment of money, people, and heat. That afternoon, a rain started, an unyielding downpour that dropped in lines so straight you wouldn't get wet if you had an umbrella. The rain cooled off the burning city.

I sat on the porch of my room for hours, drinking pressurized cans of Murphy's Irish Stout, smoking Shuangxi cigarettes, and thinking intermittently about Miranda thousands of miles away.

The rain kept up, on and off, for 36 hours. I pulled on my army coat and went to a coffee shop down in Central. The antibiotics had kicked in and already I could listen to music on my headphones. I corresponded with the guitarist from The Lovesong, over email, asking him what it was like to be in a band in Hong Kong. He suggested that without a culture of going to clubs to see bands play, the average local would rather spend money on movies or karaoke. This sentiment was echoed by Spike at *Hong Kong Magazine*, who said that just like anywhere else, people going out barhopping are into drinking, getting laid.

I returned to the Wan Chai District to experience a show being promoted by a group called The Underground. The venue looked like a rundown disco, the kind of place where people once danced but now where neighborhood drunks took residence in the bar stools while the old structure of the club remained intact around them. The place filled with a mixed crowd: fashionable Hong Kongers milling about in their narrow jeans and boutique-store t-shirts, a collection of white expats wearing button-downs without ties, and a few shady types hovering closely around the bar, wondering why the young folks had invaded their corner haunt.

I had missed the first band but I was in time for a group called The David Bowie Knives. The article about this show had placed significant praise on this band and so I pushed forward toward the center of the crowd. It hit us: heavy guitars, Black Sabbath-style, and extended jamming. It just wallowed in the same place, one loud hard-rock jam that seemed appropriate for three married men in their basement on a Sunday afternoon. The band itself consisted of three middle-aged white guys. They seemed to be enjoying it. The crowd loved it.

I once saw Wynton Marsalis do a live Q&A after a performance at West High School in Iowa City. A teenager asked him how he felt about contemporary music. Wynton said, "We are living in an ignorant age." He recalled his youth and playing in a funk band with his brother, Branford, in the early '70s. He said they were in the background playing their horns and up front it was mayhem—"There were guitarists jumping off the stage, going crazy, going wild."

Branford turned to Wynton and said, "It's going to get worse, brother, and you're going to live to see it."

He wasn't just referring to the wild funk jams they were playing in that band but to what they saw as the entire degradation of music and the way that we, the people, would readily consume and eat it up. To be sure, Wynton Marsalis has often expressed elitist views of what is good and bad in music, but there was a real universal truth in what he was attempting to illuminate: we wanted music as crass entertainment and we wanted to get laid.

"We are living in an ignorant age," Wynton repeated—almost an apology to all humanity, "I am sorry. We are living in an ignorant age."

6

There was a spider on the wall of my room at the university and it was so big I wanted to vomit. I wished it hadn't rained for so long; I reckoned that was the only reason it had come inside. I would have liked to leave it alone but with its plump stomach and arms that stretched like freshly sharpened pencils I was too afraid to fall asleep with it living in my room. I was also too afraid to kill it. I couldn't even get near. I considered hitting it with a newspaper or a large book and imagined its interiors opening up all over the wall. If it had touched me I would have evaporated. Then I fantasized about it talking, telling me to be its slave. It wanted to poke me with its long tentacle arms as I squirmed in its web. It was a low moment for me: I was too scared to kill it and too scared to let it be. It moved into the bathroom and just watching it walk that short distance made me dizzy. I left my room and checked my email. I scrolled through the messages, hoping to suspend my acknowledgement of the spider's existence. There was nothing new from my contacts. I smiled at other people checking their email in the computer lab.

When I got back to the room the spider had worked its way into the shower. I looked at it closely, every grotesque ridge on its back. I turned on the shower full force, all the way to red: I was going to steam it to death. It was so strong, so resistant—its legs working up the sides of the shower despite the increasing moisture on the tiles. It knew this was life or death. As it struggled I grew sicker: sick with the sight of this monster, sick with myself for torturing it into a grave when I could have executed it with one clean swipe. As it pushed its feet against the walls and eventually slid down to the drain I felt the grotesqueness seeping away from the spider's ravaged body and into my bones. I was the monster.

Lying there at the edge of the drain, it was looking up at me, begging me to stop. It knew it wouldn't make it now: it just wanted me to leave it alone, to let it die in peace. I thought it over and an irrational fear deep inside of me said that if I let the thing live, it would go back to its nest, recuperate, and plot its revenge, coming to me later in the night and biting a hole out of my chest, infecting me with spider-rabies. I noticed a can of roach killer on top of the toilet. In a final, desperate act, I unleashed a half-can of roach poison on the spider.

It gave in, gave up, and coughed out its last stroke of life. I felt like a piece of shit. I crumpled up a huge wad of toilet tissue, picked up the carcass, and tossed it in the toilet. I had failed some major life test. Either I was supposed to let the thing live or kill it with honorable grace. I did neither. I abused it like a helpless prisoner of war, prodding its body with degradations. I wanted to hop on a bus, go back downtown and drink, lose myself in the thrust of the city and its endless inebriations.

The masks we wear on a daily basis are absurd.

I looked at Miranda, one day in the late spring, sitting peacefully on her bed, quietly plucking away at her laptop, and I knew then that we would not stay together forever. Our separation—whether it happened in days, months, or years—was inevitable. I knew it was over. She glanced up at me and smiled.

I smiled back. I displayed affection.

I crept forward down the path of an extinct relationship. If we are to be honest people, I wonder, is that the point at which we should sever our ties—the point when we know it is over? Should we stand up and say, at the risk of emotional carnage, that everything is finished, that we must let go? Do we stand up and walk out of the room, leaving everything behind, not looking back? If we are weak people, do we smile in the face of impending dissolution and continue making breakfasts, watching movies, sharing beds, and holding hands because for all that we want to walk away from, there is still that glowing morsel that first drew us in that we are too afraid to leave behind forever? We made breakfasts. We watched movies. We shared beds. We held hands. Our small love was a dark cloud, an impending storm painted over with brushstrokes of denial.

7

We left Hong Kong for several days to visit the island of Macau. We took a ferry west. The change in location occurred in tandem with my personal descent into digestive failure. I caught a stomach bug and it was headstrong, persistent. I would eat exquisite meals—tender cuts of beef, delicately seared fish, deeply marinated fowl—and precisely 20 minutes later I would exit for relief in the washroom.

We boarded at another university but this was a hospitality school. Everything put before us was the work of a student, their bridge between apprenticeship and graduation. These meals mattered to them as much as they mattered to me. Fresh water catches and finely selected meats were at the tips of my cutlery every time I sat down for a meal in the school's restaurant. My backside erupted while my mouth indulged.

I walked around the island. My time in between post-meal disruptions and the next meal were my only peaceful moments of the day. The downtown plaza reflected the architectural footprint of Macau's former colonial occupiers, the Portuguese. Modern Chinese buildings had sprouted up in batches, towering around the Old World landmarks. There were long stretches of casinos—massive intrusions around the edges of the island. The casino companies sought to keep building them—they were beacons of escape for the mainland businessmen. Weekends of gambling had become extremely popular, almost a national pastime, particularly for Chinese men. The wealth accumulated by the Macau casinos had already surpassed the gross intake of the Vegas strip. American casino houses—MGM, Sands—strategized their invasion of this fertile, profitable land. And, beyond the casinos themselves, the additional amenities that came with them—resorts, condos, entertainment centers—were beginning to take form as well. Macau was a boomtown of pleasures. All this grandeur but my priorities remained with the identification of clean and subtle locations where I could sit down and let my insides dismantle themselves.

In my moments alone, sitting near the ruins of St. Paul's Cathedral, I sifted through my reactions to the shows I had sought out in Hong Kong. It became clear to me that I wasn't particularly fond of the music I had seen. Nor did I have the necessary inspiration to write an article about it. What would be the point? Who needed to hear about a music scene that was only half there? What was the critical benefit to anyone? And who was I to judge quality when clearly the *desire* to play music had been present in Hong Kong's fledgling indie bands? Wasn't it ultimately more important that people were trying in earnest to make and support art regardless of how the art was actually turning out? I didn't have answers but I knew that I felt out of place. Not the out-of-place foreigner in a new land, the out-of-place writer amidst a staff of music critics back home.

In the April 1993 issue of *SPIN*, editor Jim Greer penned an article called "Smells Like Scene Spirit" about a town called New Market, Virginia, where a fertile music scene had sprung up with a multitude of indie bands. This report emerged in the wake of Nirvana's multi-platinum breakthrough album *Nevermind*. The band's home-base, Seattle, had become a center of attention in the music world. Record labels hungered for the next lucrative alternative band from the underground. And they looked beyond the Pacific Northwest. They scanned the entire country, creating a major label signing rush that put a lot of advances in bands' pockets but didn't result in as many MTV superstars. Greer's article, however, was a well-designed April Fool's hoax. New Market, Virginia, exists but there wasn't actually the thriving music scene that Greer had written about. Legend maintains that, despite the joke, several representatives from major labels flew out to New Market, scouring the small town for potential signees. On the surface, Greer had written a funny joke about the blind greed of the record industry, a machine willing to go to any end to turn four friends in a basement into a million-dollar profit. Going deeper, Greer had also commented on "us" as a whole, our inexplicable need as consumers and self-appointed cultural critics to find and define the music world through the discovery of new scenes.

I tried to write, to stitch together my observations into something that would pass safely across my editor's desk, but nothing came out. I was hungry to discover—to be the one who had discovered—but I didn't know why.

Miranda giddily invited me over to her apartment one day in the spring. She had news. I squeezed through her small doorway. We were always cramped, always kneeling. She told me that she had been invited to interview for a library position at the prestigious college in the Rust Belt. One of my high school teachers had gone there. All of those small private schools—the Gettysburgs, Oberlins, Dickinsons—gelled together as a fortified stereotype in my mind. I imagined cheery white students walking around with backpacks, North Face fleeces, and baseball caps with the names of their schools printed across the front and whichever Division III sports team they played for—lacrosse, field hockey, football—scribbled in smaller print on the line below. There would be keggers in rundown houses, drunken petting in bathrooms with dusty, grimy toilet seats, and periodic streaking across open fields after the first snowfall of the season. People would graduate with respectable degrees in history, English, and chemistry. There would be the occasional faces of color sifting around campus, their billowing presence somehow always captured in the photographs of admissions pamphlets and websites. All the while, people like Miranda would toil in the libraries, ensuring that student research would fall back on the best books, periodicals, and electronic databases.

"That is wonderful," I said.

"I know, I know!" She was smiling, genuinely happy. To even get the interview she had achieved something remarkable. There were no jobs at that time for people with master's degrees—it seemed possible there would never be jobs for them again. University budgets had shrunk in parallel with the depressed economy of the impending Great Recession. Most of her classmates would be filling out applications at bars, restaurants, and cafés while a few would be so lucky to get interviews at distinguished liberal arts colleges or universities. The parameters of the job market couldn't have been any more apparent. If you got a job, you took it. It didn't matter if it was in Manhattan, Anchorage, or Hattiesburg, you always took the job. They were both desperate and opportune times: if the career path you had picked for stability had bleak prospects you could alternately simply choose to follow the real dream you had harbored all along.

I asked her generic questions about the nature of the job and what she would need to do to prepare for the interview. She was excited, her eyes radiant. I realized—embarrassed that I hadn't realized it before—that she wasn't often happy. She moved through her days as if she had settled, left something behind—her art?—in exchange for something more stable, more acceptable and passable to the rest of the world around her. I congratulated her, I kissed her, and we both refused to discuss the notion that her getting the job would spell out the precise negotiations of our demise. I envisioned an exit strategy, a fight waiting to happen.

8

We returned from Macau and our program ended. Students finalized plans to head back to the States or further abroad. I stayed, slowly waiting for everyone to evaporate so that I could dig further into my fruitless attempts to understand the island's elusive culture of music. I felt compelled by duty if not by passion. A creative writing professor from the University of Hong Kong liked the idea of me writing about local music. She put me in touch with her friend, Allen Youngblood, an American jazz musician living in Hong Kong. He had his own sextet and held the title of music director at the Foreign Correspondents' Club (FCC). He invited me to meet him there for an interview.

Located near the populist bars of Lan Kwai Fong, the FCC was a private organization drawing its membership from the international media, diplomats, and business people. It cost anywhere from HK$2,000–HK$10,000 (~$250–$1250) to join, depending on whether you were a real journalist or just someone who wanted to be associated with the club. Then there was a HK$950/month fee (~$120) that all members paid to maintain their status. Like most social clubs it provided an opportunity for people, especially businessmen, to engage with potential partners. It also helped establish one's class stature in Hong Kong. If you were not a member but still in suit-wearing circles you might feel like an outsider.

When I arrived I asked the bartender if I could get a drink. He almost laughed at me. "Members only, sir."

"But I'm with Mr. Youngblood," I said.

He shook his head, put a glass of ice-water in front of me, and worked on someone else's cocktail. I sat on a barstool and doodled random notes in my journal, attempting to pass the time with a projected sense of purpose. Allen Youngblood arrived 30 minutes later and immediately told the bartender I was okay. The bartender's demeanor shifted. He asked me, with a genuine smile, what I wanted to drink.

Youngblood was black. He had a bald head. Not too many black people to be seen on the streets let alone in a place like the FCC. When we met and shook hands we bonded immediately, the necessary bond of two black men wandering a foreign land alone. His voice was loud and comforting.

"Check this out," he said. "We got another brother here in this club."

The bartender smiled because it was his job to smile at the jokes of the club members.

Youngblood was a piano player who had been in Hong Kong since 1992 when he moved from Seattle. He wore linen khakis and a loose shirt. Sunglasses hung casually over the bridge of his nose. It wasn't that bright in the club. We were in the basement lounge. Little groups of expats sat around tables, eating dinner, drinking booze. There were a few loners at the bar. Periodically, they picked their faces up from the pools of their drinks and looked around the lounge.

Youngblood pointed to an old American guy with white hair. "That motherfucker's been here since Vietnam. Just showed up and stayed." The bartender hovered over me, his smile inviting and coercive.

"Yes," I said. "Another drink, please."

There were groups of them apparently, the writers and photojournalists who had covered the Vietnam War and then come back to Hong Kong to regroup in between assignments. The club became their refuge, a place where they could enjoy their whiskey and not be bothered by VC bullets shattering their tumblers. Youngblood told me he came to Hong Kong and stayed because he got a one-off tour job playing jazz piano overseas. That gig turned into more work. He liked it and stayed, eventually got the invitation to be musical director of the FCC. He was responsible for making sure a band played in the downstairs lounge every night. A few nights a week, his combo would come down and play. Other nights he found different jazz groups or solo acts to fill in the gaps. The solo acts, he said, were "dudes with an acoustic guitar" playing the hits. "Folk music," he said. "What was popular when they were young in the '60s and '70s." This meant Buffalo Springfield, Joni Mitchell, and The Eagles. He also booked an annual jazz festival at the club as well as a holiday gala that had featured acts like The Temptations and Blondie. The job allowed him to make his own music and do it exactly as he liked. I asked him what kind of records he made.

"Weird shit," he said. "Can't always be playing that stuff down here."

I wondered if, ultimately, cutting avant-garde records in Hong Kong exposed his work to roughly the same amount of people that doing the same thing in the States would have done. A small experimental club like The Stone in New York couldn't fit more than a hundred people. What did it mean to play for a hundred people in Hong Kong instead of a hundred in the States? Did it even matter or was the fact that he played at all—was that the only thing that counted in the end?

Youngblood had taken his sextet around Asia and to Australia. His drummer was American too, a tall black guy who had also been playing in Seattle. "Yeah, he came over when I came," Youngblood said, laughing. "He stayed too."

I kept thinking how funny or revolutionary it was, these two guys playing in the American scene and then they head here to do their own thing. Scene as self. Scene as portable. Scene-free.

Youngblood shook my hand as he stood up to leave. "Good luck with this story, man. Send me a copy when you're done." He walked off and left me with the tab.

I looked at the bartender. He smiled and took my card.

9

Miranda excelled at her job interview. When she returned she talked at length about the beauty of the campus and the surrounding area. A rich wooded landscape surrounded the college town, which had been built in the late 18th century. I imagined the extended route of travel from Iowa—at least two airplanes and a long car ride. To leave Iowa and move further into rural oblivion seemed impossible, yet it could happen.

It is difficult to understand the process of falling out of love. How much of it is circumstantial, how much of it is inevitable in spite of the situation, and how much of it just happens by chance changes in the hearts of those who made the pact? I wondered if I had misread my own desires, if I was the type of person who fell into relationships irresponsibly just because I needed someone or something to hold on to. When I had first met Miranda, the surge of passion in my core had been palpable. Her very presence had dizzied me. It wasn't a mere physical attraction, a late-night wink across a bar after several drinks that leads to one night of romance, but rather a fully rendered spell, lengthy and thorough in its consumption. I had felt connected to her and deemed it inevitable that I would follow that connection to its source. Is it possible that I didn't like what I found when I eventually got there—the beautiful, responsible woman who had turned her back on art, the woman who didn't seem happy on her own, who needed a pillar, the woman whom I was incapable of pleasing in bed yet stayed with me nonetheless? Perhaps I was stunned by my own inadequacies both physical and spiritual. The realization that I could not will myself into the mold of a reasonable partner was a crushing blow. My self-hate infected me quickly and rudely. I turned it back at her; I resonated with disgust at our faulty bond. I wanted to separate, move on. We fail. We try again. And we fail. We are unable to grasp the future until we look at ourselves honestly and regard the truths we have buried systematically and forcefully in the bowels of our souls. Miranda asked me how often I would visit if she took the job, assuming bluntly that our relationship would continue over great distances. I sat silently, for I could not utter the real answer. I wouldn't visit. We would break up.

"I don't know," I said. "As much as I can."

A few weeks passed, the school made an offer, and she took the job. I was leaving soon for Hong Kong at the end of the spring. When I returned I would work and write in Berkeley for the summer. When I came back to Iowa City she would already be gone, her mark, her influence scrubbed from the streets, the bars, the bedrooms. We sat on her bed, discussing this blank future. Our long arms stretched across the sheets, our hands intertwining at the center of the bed, radiating with tension. Even fate had promised us nothing, with me going halfway across the world and her impending departure encroaching. What was there to say? There was only a dull pain to face and I had hoped that we could resign to begin facing it, letting it set in.

"Don't you dare break up with me," Miranda said. I recoiled from her.

"I can't do long distance."

"You aren't even willing to give it a try?"

"I just can't. It won't work." What I was too afraid to tell her was that I didn't love her *enough* to maintain our relationship over the distance.

"If I was still here, would we be dating?"

"Yeah," I said, but even then I doubted how long that engagement would last. I had already been pulling up my stakes. It was a matter of time until the tent collapsed. Our love was the tent, this you understand, but I should emphasize that it was becoming a very, very small tent, barely big enough for more than a single occupant. And we were both tall people. I could see the end so clearly—why was her vision obscured by fog?

"If we would be together while I'm here," she said, "then we will be together when I'm there."

"I can't do it," I said again. I held my ground but only slightly. My footing was weak. I considered giving in. It somehow seemed more palatable to endure the ache of lingering unhappiness than to face the wild eruption that was brimming beneath the surface.

"You are so fucking selfish," she said.

Her statement sheared right through me, exposing my nerves. Another question emerged: Why would anyone want a man like this, a man like me? And yet she clung to what little we had—our union a symbol that would keep her moving forward.

I failed her. I failed myself.

I agreed to a plan and we laid out its details. She would move to the Rust Belt. I would return to Iowa City in the fall. We would be separate. We would continue dating. It was a terrible decision but it was a decision I had helped to make. Ultimately, I had been unable to slice the cord, to let go, to watch someone perish under the weight of a collapsed heart and to know that I was the one who had broken it, and in that sense I was being extremely selfish. I was a reticent boxer who couldn't end the fight, who couldn't throw the final punch. The conclusion itself hadn't been evasive or sly. It was me who had run away.

10

I lounged on the edge of a bed in the hotel I had checked into for my final days in the city. It was small but at least it was quiet. Somewhere on the streets of Hong Kong someone was selling a pig or a camera or a cell phone. All I could do was sit and listen to the hum of the fan in the bathroom. My shades were drawn. Narrow hints of light crossed into the room. I was entirely unafraid of solitude.

It was my last night in town. I sat on the toilet in the bathroom and read *Hong Kong Magazine*. I resolved to see one more show before leaving. Spike sent me an email.

"The best thing about the scene," he wrote, "is that it exists at all, that there are people interested in playing this stuff and people interested in checking it out. I suppose so long as it remains resolutely non-commercial, it will remain a primarily underground phenomenon."

At The Underground show people definitely had fun. It didn't matter that the classic rock dullness of The David Bowie Knives was uninspiring. People were excited because their friends and acquaintances were onstage actually doing something with their lives beyond the corporate machinery that makes Hong Kong synonymous with any big Western city or Mainland China hub—Spike himself was a self-described American expat working at a company as a "mindless drone." The music scene, which he admitted sometimes "sucked," was still his "lifeline."

I went to the Fringe Club. It was slick and dark, its walls painted black. There was a bar in the back and a stage up front. I got there early and sat alone drinking Carlsberg. By the time a band called J.O.Y. started playing, the place had begun to fill up with a mix of local hipsters and expats. I moved to the front, raring for this last foray into the city's music world. J.O.Y.'s sound was overblown. There were too many musicians doing too little. They crowded the small confines of the stage. I tried to hold on for a few songs. The synthesizer blasted a fake horn sound that made me cringe. I cowered away, covering my ears. I couldn't win. The music didn't want me to win.

I migrated to the nearby Lan Kwai Fong and went into a bar distended with expats. Walking into that bar was like skateboarding drunk across a fault line. The earth would shift and I would be absorbed into its cavernous cracks. Men and women danced jaggedly, without care for appearance. The sound of the Cantopop band exploded from the stage. Every cover song supplanted the original with such earnest interpretation. This was dance music for hungry people, people on the hunt. And what other animals in the kingdom of life hunt each other so cunningly and violently as two human beings out for carnivorous, wild sex? We consume our prey and in the same moment our own bodies are split open and devoured. A snake salting its own tail. A liar eating his own shit made up as a finely sauced bistro steak. A disciple sacrificing himself to a god in his own image.

I ordered myself a beer.

A woman grabbed me. She was solid and real like a pillar. She wore a short haircut, maybe a middle-aged decision to let go of the long locks of her 20s and 30s. She didn't have a wedding ring. I read her years through the creases around her eyes, the booze-tinged rosiness of her nose, and the thin, tight purse of her lips. Her dark dress hung loosely over her body, hiding the curves that accentuated themselves with age. Though, when she moved, her bust displayed prominently and affectionately like an advertisement for something that you knew you already wanted to buy.

She put a shot down on the bar and said, "This is for you, love."

I forced it down my throat.

"Come dance," she said. She had bought me a drink. I owed her at least one dance.

I absorbed the rhythm of the song unabashedly. I can't remember the tune: feel free to insert the cover of your choice—"Born in the U.S.A.," "Like a Virgin," "No Diggity"—it doesn't really matter, any pop song will do. Just imagine the freedom with which you would dance to said song in the privacy of your apartment, volume cranked, on a Friday night, that first bottle of Syrah swaying back and forth in your hand because, fuck it, it's Friday and you don't need a wine glass, you just need a drink and the damn bottle will suffice. My partner smiled, exposing her set of manicured teeth. I succumbed to the insistent call of Cantopop. I forgot, in an instant, all of the indie bands I had tried to track down. I dismissed the power of original expression and substituted it with the notion of just having a good time. She pulled me in, closer to her body. I felt the presence of her curves, the soft, pliant acceptance of her flesh. I advanced my hands around her waist, holding her firmly, then working up to her back and shoulders. We kissed. I had fallen. Miranda's heart stuttered briefly thousands of miles away. The music held me, expanding its grip around my body. Damn my search for the underground, my pretentious and presumptuous estimations about a culture that was not my own. Cantopop, amidst all of the loud guitars and independent creative impulses, had ultimately conquered me. I caved into the familiar sounds, into my usual patterns. I pulled my face back from the mouth of my dance partner.

I went to the bathroom. White men—Brits, Aussies, Kiwis—hovered about me. They were pissing, laughing, and drinking—navigating that small bathroom like it was the deck of a party cruise. They were loud and happy and quickly becoming forgetful, the iron curtains of blackouts falling down curtly behind their eyes. I went back to the bar and signaled for a beer. I looked around and painfully acknowledged I didn't have any friends there. When I was at my worst, I was always at it alone. I felt her hand around my waist. I put the beer to my mouth and turned around. She was smiling, she was waiting, she was ready. I put the beer down on the bar.

She lived in a one-bedroom apartment close to the fancy bar district. I think she worked in commercial banking. The apartment reflected wealth: designer furniture, an elegant, modern bed, and an exquisite marble-top island in her kitchen. She tossed me onto the bed and I pulled her down on top of me. We wrestled back and forth, our mouths locked on each other's bodies—on our mouths, our chests, our stomachs, our sex. Our clothes lay serenely on the floor. She reached for a condom in her bedside drawer. She tore open the package and handed me the instrument.

I marveled at the sheer velocity at which our bodies came together. Quick, ferocious intervals, both militant and tribal. Pushing back and forth—we were both starving for something, clawing at each other to see if we could get it. She held my arms with a brutal grip every time she climaxed. It felt as if she was drawing something out of me. The sweat dripped from my face onto hers and I sunk in periodically to kiss her cheeks, her lips, her neck. I looked down the length of our bodies, watching the collision, and noticed that the condom had disappeared. Still in motion, I told her what I had seen. She clutched my head and brought my ear close to her lips. "It's all right, love. It's all right." Even then I didn't know her name.

I awoke in the aftermath, our bodies lying naked in her bed. The stillness of her apartment jarred me. Beyond the apartment walls, the enduring thrall of Hong Kong—the cars, the people, the industry—chugged along. I had no inkling of time, only my impending responsibilities: checking out of my hotel, killing some hours, and catching my flight back to the States. I washed my face in her bathroom and put on my clothes. She lay there, happily absorbed by sleep. I left her as she had first found me in the bar: alone.

Outside, the heat punished me. It colluded with my hangover in an effort to bring me to my knees, but I trudged along the streets, almost holding on to the walls of buildings as I found my way back to the hotel. My movements were instinctual, the geography of the city had seeped, if only slightly, into my system and somehow I knew which direction to follow in order to get home. I was disheveled, my appearance torn to shreds. The hotel people barely noticed me. Perhaps this was the way of tourists: victims of drink, Cantopop, and sex. I sat on the toilet in my room and something vile came out. It felt like the last shards of whatever had hid inside of me and died. I tried to pack my huge suitcase but every configuration proved a challenge. Somehow I had amassed so much crap—new clothes, books, and knick-knacks—that the suitcase proved impossible to pack. I wasn't this kind of tourist, I didn't buy things to bring home, but the length of the trip had worn me down. Finally, I was able to push down on the top of my suitcase and hold it there long enough to force the zippers around the perimeter. I hauled it down to the lobby. I told them I would leave it there and pick it up later. They seemed to agree.

I walked to one of the big malls downtown. There was a huge one with stores that unfolded on top of each other. The mall was clean and bright and packed. I had showered but I did not feel clean. I passed by a movie theater and looked at the titles. I wanted to see one. It would eat away the hours. I could pass the time with a glowing story in front of my eyes. I wouldn't have to think about my own life. I sat in the lobby for some time and just waited. People flowed into the theater, one after the other. People flowed out. People just walked by poking into other stores, into more and more commerce. My head hurt and my body sagged, but the machine kept moving. I thought about seeing a movie again but I couldn't make myself do it. Something inside of me had stalled.

On the passageways that connected the buildings and malls, there were Filipino families congregating. I heard they came out on Sundays for urban picnics. It was a social time for them, an escape from the hard weeks many of them had endured, working long hours in domestic service to the Chinese. They were house cleaners, nannies, and cooks and this was their one day off. It was like American slaves getting their church on a Sunday. Locals had told me that some Chinese looked down on these people—that they were seen as less pure. Their skin was darker and that was a mark against them. Even the Chinese had their disenfranchised brown people.

The evening approached and I returned to the hotel to pick up my things and make my way to the airport. The brutality of my hangover had subsided with the day but I was left with a dull feeling of regret, a heavy, grey post-alcohol depression. I knew I was upset about so many things but it would take work to pull them out from my interior and identify all that was wrong. The airport buzzed with energetic passengers coming and going from the big city. It was as alive as the Hong Kong streets inside that massive hub of travel.

I waited in line as people slowly checked in for the international flight. I was tired and emitting a clammy sweat from my pores, the routine escape of poisons from a polluted body.

A woman took my ticket, at first smiling then turning placid after she had scanned my appearance, finding me to be a mediocre specimen, turned on myself by too much failure, too much time in the city. She kept asking questions, simple inquiries, about my travel, but I had trouble computing and responding to her in appropriate measures.

"Sir," she said, "your passport, please."

I stared beyond her eyes, through them, through the thick stone walls of the airport onto the distant runways and darkened night sky.

"Your passport, please," she said.

Something clicked and I tried to smile as I turned over my identification. She took a long time processing my information, plucking away on her computer. I leaned on her counter, exhausted and sweaty, hoping I would just roll up and die. I couldn't stay any longer and didn't have the energy to make it back home. There was a ringing at the back of my head. The woman was calling out to me.

"Your bag, sir," she said. I caught her sharp eyes. I looked behind me. I was holding up the line. I hated being that person. I put my bag on the metal tray. Her eyes exploded when she saw how much it weighed.

"You must pay, sir."

"Excuse me?"

"You must pay. Your weight is too much."

I looked at my suitcase bulging to capacity. I understood what she meant. I dropped to my knees, opening my carryon, pushing items about to see if I could make room in it and lighten the load of my suitcase. I reluctantly opened the suitcase, afraid it would never close again. Behind me, I could feel the tension of those other international travelers. *Why doesn't he just give them his credit card and get the fuck out of the way?* I hurriedly tried to shift pieces of clothing into my carryon. Sweat poured down my face. Toxins, embarrassment, over-exertion. I stuffed the carryon and now I could barely close it. I tossed it to the side. I leaned my entire weight on the top of the suitcase and worked the zipper around, forcing it closed. I put it back on the metal tray, just staring at it, and then beyond it toward the rows of bags slipping away on the conveyer belt.

A couple behind me rolled their eyes. Behind them, a tall executive in a suit tapped his watch, his motions seeming to curse the skinny, ragged black man on the floor of the airport. The airline lady leaned down to my lowly position on the floor and continued to scold me, her comments repeating, her sharp Cantonese accent echoing in my ear. I tried to understand her but I didn't even understand myself. *Sir, you must pay. You have too much. You're trying to leave with more than you came.*

No Country

"That we are in the midst of a crisis is now well understood," the new president had said earlier at the inauguration to nearly two million people in Washington, D.C. The economic crisis clawed at the nation's confidence. The Great Recession loomed. It was Inauguration Day 2009 and we were in Iowa City. The race had started in Iowa the previous year with the primary caucus. Barack Obama secured a victory in that first, essential contest and many Iowans took pride in the part they had played to launch his pursuit of the presidency. It was late now and we were in the bar. Ethan and Jeffrey practiced lines for their play and I was closing down the back. I washed pint glasses and scrubbed surfaces, lifted stools and turned them upside down on top of the bar.

Ethan leaned into Jeffrey, who was much shorter, and said, "You almost there. Now say that shit like it's natural." Ethan was playing Miles Davis and Jeffrey was John Coltrane. The play was scheduled to open in a few days in a small black box theater on campus. We would all be there tucked into seats, watching our friends succeed. Jeffrey wasn't even an actor. He was an undergraduate writer who read books and drank too much. Ethan had failed to find enough black actors in Iowa City to act in his play about the life of Miles Davis. When he was casting a couple of months earlier, he had come up to me in the bar, laughing, "Dre, we gotta find some niggas or this play gonna be some one-man show shit."

Becca walked toward us from the front bar where it was still open and rowdy. She stumbled into us and wrapped her arms around Ethan and me. "My two favorite black people in

Iowa City," she said, looking up at us through her red bangs. Jeffrey swayed in the background, clenching his fists, looking down at his shoes—trying to hold on to his character.

"Fucked up, right?" I said. "It's inauguration day and all of the black people are hanging out in the back of the bar." We laughed and Becca walked past us into the back room. I fed the fish and turned off the lights. Up front, people were less noisy now. The bar had closed and it was the after-hours crew. I walked to the front, poured a beer, and took a seat on a stool. The warm lights behind the bar illuminated the bottles of whiskey, vodka, and gin. I knew I should head home and write but I decided to indulge the evening with old friends.

The ritual began with a neat shot of Tullamore D.E.W. Ethan spoke with reverence for August Wilson, his favorite playwright. He slapped his hand on the bar, his voice heavy with experience and hope and said, "Damn, we gotta get out there and make something good." By *there* he meant the world.

I hugged him. He laughed and looked at Becca and pointed for another round of whiskey. Ethan had grown up in Chicago. He wore that legacy proudly though he had left the city to go to college. He said it had been a necessary step—an escape. He loved his home: the Bears, the White Sox, and the South Side. And he also understood the value of leaving all of that behind. Chicago had borne out so many children stripped of possibility and privilege and Ethan honored the rare luck and determination that had helped him evade a less fortunate path.

My mother had also grown up in Chicago. Her mother had extradited them from Jim Crow Texas when she was eight years old in the early 1950s. Other members of their family had relocated to Chicago much earlier, part of a robust migration that witnessed the city's black population increase from 40,000 in 1910 to almost 300,000 by 1940. Redlines had determined my family's geographical fate. Through racially-motivated "covenant laws" Chicago had infamously constructed a "Black Belt" that limited its black population to specific neighborhoods. My mother lived in Bronzeville. Like Ethan, she loved Chicago and the rich spirit of her neighborhood despite the subtler racism of Northern segregation. And yet she would also escape in order to find her success. She would seek opportunity elsewhere, moving beyond the city's imposed limitations for black people. She would move from one kind of isolation to another.

Ethan was relaxed now, sitting on a barstool, his head bent down to his whiskey glass. He smiled and said Jeffrey would pull it off. It would be one of Ethan's last plays as a theater student at the University of Iowa. He didn't even ask if I'd be there but rather which night. It was part of our code. Black artists supported other black artists. Perhaps such obligations existed everywhere else in the country, but it felt especially important there in the heart of a cold Midwestern winter.

On the way home I passed a group of young drunks pushing each other around: a portrait of Iowa City, the college town. A black guy grimaced back at a large white kid. Another black kid held the white kid back and he was laughing. The white kid was bursting, "C'mon, let me just talk to your boy. We'll settle this shit out."

The black kid was still laughing, holding him back, "Naw, man, I think you better go home."

I didn't like this part of the walk, floating past the lowest common denominator bars, where boys brewed outside just past closing time. They had failed to find resolution in the grip of alcohol and now they wanted to fight.

Down the road, away from the clamor of the bars and into the calm hum of residential living, I approached a boy and a girl, drunk and bumping into each other as they walked. They stopped abruptly on the sidewalk. The girl was apparently trying to remember exactly which house she lived in. I passed them, my shoulder sliding lightly across the boy's jacket. "Oh pardon me," he said, his voice aggravated and taunting.

"No worries," I said and kept walking.

As I pulled farther away, he called out, "Obama's going to be a great president, right?"

I answered him but I didn't turn around, "I guess we'll have to wait and see."

They kept talking, but now to themselves. "Are you a liberal?" the girl asked him, as if the answer to this question would determine whether they spent the night together.

"Ha," he said. "I am so conservative."

I could hear them walk up the stairs of her porch. She said something but I couldn't make it out. I imagined uneasiness in the tone of her voice, a quick moment of hesitation before she committed to slipping out of her clothes and into his arms.

At home I sunk into the covers of my bed—my thoughts atmospheric from the drinks I had consumed in the last hours of the bar. My computer sat on a white wooden desktop, static and cold. I thought of the book that lay within it—thousands of words and ideas that had yet to cohere into a vision that could be shared or considered by anyone else but me. It was wholly unclear how long the process would take. But for those last moments of the night I was at peace with the uncertainty. Soon, the president would be the only black man in the whitest house in America. The winter held steady outside, insistent in its rough grasp of the flat lands.

I was asked to be on a panel at a writers' conference. They titled the panel something like "Writing the Midwest" and they wanted a short lecture about what it meant to be a Midwestern writer. I had only moved to the Midwest to pursue an MFA. I had really wanted to go to New York but it was too expensive. So if getting the degree in the Midwest made me a Midwestern writer, then okay, I could assume that role, but I felt a bit like an actor publicly presenting myself as such. I wondered, in earnest, what I would have to say about being a writer in the

Midwest. I thought of race. Or, more accurately, I wondered if the people in the room, watching our panel, would be thinking of race, would want to hear something about race because that was a script with which we had all become familiar. Would I be expected to speak about what it meant to be a black writer in the Midwest? Whatever the expectation, I questioned if it would be clichéd to bring up the idea of myself as a black writer. Wouldn't people look at me and see quite clearly that I was a black writer and, upon hearing that I was from Iowa City, wouldn't they understand that I was also a black writer from Iowa City? Wasn't that enough? Deeper inside, I knew it would be dishonest to ignore my skin, for it affects me wherever I go. If I didn't bring it up at all they would say, "Does this man even know that he's black? Is he so traumatized by the Midwest that he's forgotten who he is?" There's nothing worse than a room full of white people asking me to acknowledge my blackness. They are really just asking me to acknowledge their own expectations of my blackness—and in doing so they are very, very quietly calling me out—exposing me when I would rather just fit in.

Ethan and I called back and forth to each other on late drunken nights: *Make your shit.* We wrapped each other around the shoulders. *You better get home and make your shit.* And by *shit* we meant *art.* Better make your art. There was an implied *nigga,* hanging invisibly at the end of that phrase. You better make your art, *nigga.* There were so few of us out there that we felt a pressure to succeed, from our parents, from our friends back home, and from the deans' offices that had lured us there with fellowships. But the story was not new: black artists in white spaces, looking for recognition—alone and isolated, almost like expatriates. I have always felt like I am on the outside, even in crowded American cities like New York and San Francisco where cultures bleed over each other, where it's no surprise to see groups of blacks, whites, Latinxs, Middle Easterners, Asians, gays, straights, and unknowns milling about the subway station maybe even talking to each other and holding hands.

When I lived in San Francisco in my 20s in the early 2000s, I felt especially alone pacing the streets of the Mission or climbing the avenues of Nob Hill where I frequented dive bars, drinking with strangers, erasing myself from expectations. I was a writer and a musician. I was a refugee from the East Coast where I had grown up and gone to college. The Northeastern ritual had choked me and to loosen the bonds I had moved west to a foreign place, which promised some form of bohemian respite. I hung out with other musicians, writers, and artists. They were supposed to be elevated, enlightened creatures of an ever-impending urban renaissance, wielding their post-modern paint brushes, their lyric prose, their mutated guitars, and retro-futuristic fashion. But there is nothing like sitting in a room of well-educated and cultured white folk and hearing someone say the word *nigger*—not using it as an insult but bringing up the term, in some abstract capacity, to discuss it intellectually as if the contexts of theory and rhetoric take away the fatal edges of a hurtful word. What's worse, the intentional racist or the unknowing one? Sitting there in that marvelously diverse city I was still a black man hovering around a large group of self-proclaimed outsiders. I was on the outside of the outside. I was freezing.

Despite its vast mix of people, San Francisco embraced segregation: stark separations across lines of money, skin, sexuality, and ethnicity. If you walked the streets intently you could see the cities within the cities: Asian American populations in Chinatown, Richmond, and the Sunset; Latinxs in the Mission and pockets farther south; the destitute in the Tenderloin; the blacks in Bayview-Hunters Point; and the gay men in the Castro. Yet even these segregated districts experienced no safety from eventual conquest: The growth opportunities in the Mission glistened brightly in the eyes of urban prospectors. Buildings that couldn't be easily vacated for new projects might mysteriously burn to the ground only to resurface as modern structures with affluent occupants more fitting for the neighborhood's rising property values.

As a pioneering tram line stretched from the ballpark down 3rd Street, the previously unseemly Bayview-Hunters Point braced for the pending storms of annex and renewal. It had been a public housing development south of downtown in the 1920s and welcomed an influx of African American residents during and after World War II. For several years, it existed as an interracial community with a lively business district running along 3rd Street. After the war, the black population increased significantly as redlining and white residents' reluctance to have black migration into other neighborhoods in San Francisco forced the home-seekers into the public housing developments in Bayview. In the 1950s urban renewal pushed black residents out of the Fillmore District, with many of them relocating to Bayview. By 1968, the neighborhood was 97% black.

I was black but, during my San Francisco years, I didn't live in Bayview. My privilege—class and education—offered me passage to live among various stratifications of the white world: 21st Century Passing. I moved first to the Haight, then Dolores Park, and finally, the Mission. Despite my artistic leanings, I maintained a steady job and I had gone to the right schools. San Francisco was always comfortable with its Pre-Approved Negroes, those who knew enough about the rules of the white system to not only navigate it but to tread carefully enough to not disrupt it. The existence of such Pre-Approved Negroes justified the idea of the city being truly diverse in the minds of the liberal, entitled white people who inhabited it. And they sincerely cared about their Pre-Approved People of Color, Pre-Approved Children of Immigrants, and Pre-Approved Homosexuals. The existence of these different people completed a circle the well-educated, well-meaning white people had hoped to finish on their path toward a fully realized, self-sanctioned adulthood. Our very presence made them feel like *the world was going to be okay after all.*

A dear friend of mine pulled me aside after I announced my plans to leave San Francisco for Iowa City. "Be careful," they said. They wanted to protect me from the engulfing whiteness of Iowa, a shroud that would surely overwhelm me. They told me a story about a black friend of theirs who had left California to take a professorship at the University of Iowa. The cultural solitude and discrimination had traumatized their friend, eventually leading to a departure from Iowa City. My friend implored me to make sure I knew what I was getting into before I left. In their heart, they believed they were only looking out for me. They couldn't imagine me being comfortable outside of San Francisco's protective borders.

I appreciated the warning, but I am always left to wonder why white people don't understand that we are under emotional assault almost everywhere we go. The question our defensive systems ask is not always how much whiteness surrounds us but more often what kinds of whiteness surround us. To rephrase an earlier inquiry: What's worse, the enthusiastic, purposeful racist *or* the one who thinks they are not even capable of being racist, the one who could never imagine stepping on your sensitive colored toes and is indeed offended when you have suggested they have done so?

I was nine years old and traveling with my parents in Europe. We were in an airport in France. At a kiosk my mom told me to pick up a comic book, something to keep my attention while we waited for the next plane. I saw a Tintin book. It was in French. Even if I couldn't read the words I could recognize the characters and piece together the story through pictures. My mother bought it without considering the content. It was Tintin, it was harmless. When I opened it up and began scanning the panels she looked over my shoulder and shuttered.

"Dammit," she said. Her voice was sharp. "These white people." I held the copy of *Tintin au Congo*, first published in 1931. Its images of the Congolese reflected fierce stereotypes of black Africans. The depictions fed into an iconography whose intent was to demean: A legacy of pitch-black natives running across the continent with ivory spheres for eyes and watermelon lips curved around teeth—white and crude like the broken keys of an old upright piano. My mom made me close the book and at first I thought she was going to throw it away. But then she told me to keep it. "I want you to remember this," she said.

When I moved to Iowa City my local coffee shop carried a Fair Trade blend called *Heart of Darkness*. It was extra-dark and pretty damn good, but the name struck me as dated and racist. When I saw that coffee, *Heart of Darkness*, I conjured the racist depictions of the Congolese from *Tintin au Congo*. This was not a healthy vision. I projected upon the mind of every young white college student who came into the coffee shop the notion that they had come to have their dark fantasies of Africa reaffirmed by that subversively named blend. I would walk into the coffee shop and look up at the board to see which coffees they had listed. The list was so prominently displayed that you couldn't miss it. Some days they filled the board with other blends, but on the worst days the name *Heart of Darkness* stared down at me and laughed. To be called a nigger by a coffee sign! It was as if that blend of coffee—*Heart of Darkness*—had been a challenge placed there to test my resolve in my new Midwestern geography.

I roused the attitude to ask the manager to discontinue the blend—and the sad fact that I had to feel embarrassed for demanding a necessary change was crushing. I was new to Iowa City. Why should I be the one to stand up in public and tear down a misplaced sign? The manager was shocked, caught off guard that the name could be construed as offensive. She didn't know much about imperialism nor had she read Joseph Conrad but a few days later, *Heart of Darkness* was gone. At the time I thought—of course!—these Iowans they just don't know any better: They've never seen black people before. And like that, I placed the representatives of the coffee shop in Iowa City into one recognizable group: Ignorant, isolated white folk—as if they lived not on the mainland in the veritable center of the United States but somewhere more distant like the outward edges of Alaska.

I researched *Heart of Darkness* further and the internet revealed that the coffee shop had actually ordered the blend from a company in California called Santa Cruz Coffee Roasting. Their website read, "This extra-dark roast delivers berry and dark chocolate notes in the fragrance followed by a smoky, robust and earthy flavor in the cup. Exceptionally smooth body balances out this heavy, 'jungly' coffee." I was stunned to find that *Heart of Darkness* was not a product of Iowan cultural neglect but rather of likely pot-smoking capitalists sitting on the coast, commenting on the surf, and indulging in their profitable fantasies of a dark continent. I suddenly felt separated from the welcoming arms of Iowa City, from the residual grasp of my former West Coast home, and from everything else around me. I felt like a black writer in a white town.

Just as privileged San Franciscans hold so dearly to their chests the notion that they are living in a progressive city—it's true, they are—that is so forward thinking as to make all of its diverse people welcome at all times—a false assumption—Californians at large sometimes assert the position that their entire state is a beacon of forward-thinking, inclusive culture. We might neglect to understand that its imperfect and innovative beacons—the Bay Area and Los Angeles—are not entirely representative of California: It is indeed a sprawling state that can be as conservative as it is liberal, as poor as it is rich, as dreamless as it is idealistic. We never know where we will find the worst of ourselves or, for that matter, the best. Yet, we are often so eager for categorization that we refuse to acknowledge the wild mess of our cultural geography.

One of my classmates at Iowa was an essayist named Eula Biss. She was on her way out when I arrived but she would later write at length about living in Iowa in her collection *Notes from No Man's Land*. In one essay, "Back to Buxton," she considered the seemingly harmonious existence of a racially integrated early 20th century Iowa coal town called Buxton. Various records, both legal and anecdotal, reflected equal access to housing, education, and opportunity for blacks and whites in Buxton. The unincorporated town lasted for about 30 years, finally closing in 1927, and former residents fondly recalled the lack of discrimination and segregation. One resident, Sue Williams, said, "I never heard the word segregation or knew its meaning until I moved to Chicago."

Biss posited Buxton as a possible utopia, a notion she sharply contrasted against what she saw as fissures in the 21st century diversity recruitment efforts at the University of Iowa. After reading a report in which minority students expressed disappointment in their experiences at the school, she questioned the university's intentions: Did it bring new students of color to the school to benefit those students' educational advancement or did it simply want to make the experiences of the overwhelmingly white student body appear worldly? Did the administration really care about their experiences in Iowa City or were the students of color just there to make the University of Iowa *look* like a good place? Years later, a professor I knew crossed the university's main lawn one day to find a photographer staging pictures of black and white students happily interacting—this carefully constructed façade perhaps meant for select pages on the admissions website and brochure. Pre-approved diversity tucked into the school's enlightened corners.

On a cold winter night, a mob of us graduate student writers, recovering from the intensity of workshop, bunched up into a shack of a bar called the Fox Head. We drank as a means of therapy. We bought pitchers of La Crosse and moved from booth to booth, talking to each other about the flaws of our craft. I sat down at a booth with a white fellow slightly older than me. We were both drunk but he was further gone than I was. He wasn't a student but a local. He had just filled the jukebox with a set of exquisite '60s-era Coltrane. It was late and the sound was perfect in that skeletal piecemeal setting. The horn echoed through the rickety bar and the drums rattled the thin, foggy windows. The place felt more like a trailer than a bar. The guy, who had put on Coltrane, talked at length about the beauty of the songs. He spoke to the history of the session we were listening to and illuminated the architecture behind this essential American music. And then he was silent. He sat back, his hand on his drink and his eyes glassy as the music overtook his senses. He was at peace, his guard down. He smiled and with reverence, comfort, and authority quietly said, "Damn, these niggers can play." It could have happened anywhere: Iowa City, San Francisco, or Paris but it happened in Iowa City. There I was—stuck, embarrassed—outside of the outside; my jaw tightened and my fists clenched.

"What the fuck?" I shouted at him and he looked at me, his eyes confused and astonished: He had no idea how we had ended up in a difficult situation. I was as astonished as he was. This kind of racism was like an April Fool's joke: You almost forgot it existed and then it slapped you in the face just as you had shed your defenses. I was standing in front of him, my fists level with his neck, wondering if I should hit him. He looked at me, still confused. My face was hot and my guts were in my throat. "Fuck you," I said and walked out of the bar. I didn't say goodbye to anyone, I just walked out silent and alone into the night.

My friend Simon, a black novelist, sat at the Fox Head one night, talking to some classmates. The same local man engaged him in an argument and at some point used that word—*nig-ger*. Simon grabbed the man and threw him to the ground. The atmosphere spiked into a state of emergency. Writers stood around Simon. He was about to crush the drunk man with his fists. A number of writers pulled him off the drunk who was shaken, shell-shocked, who had perhaps for the first time understood that he could risk his own safety as a result of his actions, his words. No matter how deeply the booze had sunken him into a blackout stupor, he was awake, his eyes wide open. Simon stood above him, his fists gleaming with the burden of shame, ready to strike out against someone or something for centuries of wrong-doing. Simon was impassioned with anger, volatile and violent. He was a big man, the kind of guy you wanted on your side in a situation like this, but in his day-to-day actions he was always kind, thoughtful, and encouraging. Yet, now the mostly white writers stood around him, on edge. He was no longer the Pre-Approved Negro.

I talked to Simon later about the incident. I told him that I had also come into conflict with the drunk. I told Simon how I had shouted at him and walked out of the bar. Simon pulled at my shoulders gently, "No," he said, "you were wrong. You enabled him. By not engaging him more directly, you allowed him to continue being a racist."

I tried to say something but I couldn't find the words. He had reminded me that even though we were always under attack we had to be ready to confront our opponents on a daily basis. He contended that this was our only path to real change: to face every conflict directly all the time. I thought about *Heart of Darkness* in the coffee shop and how I had talked to the management and how I had then only scoffed at the drunk for his racist comments. I had neglected to bear arms in a fight that concerned larger issues than my own well-being. I shook my head, embarrassed to look at Simon. He looked back at me—his disappointment had turned to compassion. He was a few years older than me and even in that scant difference in age, he had seen—no, he had endured—more than I had yet to experience. He knew well how these kinds of conflicts would follow us wherever we made our homes.

The bigot at the Fox Head had revealed more than the racist overtones that afflict our American towns and cities. He was not just a racist, he was also a drunkard. Many of us were. Indeed, drinking—as macabre sport, as perpetual crutch, and as reliable escape—revealed itself as one of the town's most enduring traits. There were so many different ways to lose one's self in Iowa City and drinking provided the best avenue for endless disillusionment: The worst, most confused moments came during long immersions in alcohol. Some people called Iowa City "The Black Hole." People came and never left. They couldn't get out. Was it inertia or some form of misunderstood genius? And why was it that we wanted to be lost in a holding pattern or a melody that never resolved? Booze became one of the bricks that really sunk me for a long time in Iowa City. And "sink" is to be understood in all possible forms: the booze sunk me as in to ground me and also sunk me as in to periodically 86 the progress of my writing and sunk me as in to stall my maturation into a fully realized human.

I knew I wasn't the only one: I could see so many others around me, sinking or waiting to be sunk. I saw them the moment I arrived: young writers surrounded by pitchers of beer, old writers—wasted Workshoppers—who never left, holding on to tumblers of whiskey, old men drinking anything, young college kids with ridiculous shots, post-college grads with tall pints, all of them stuck in Iowa City, just a bit too comfortable to move away from the warm beds they had made for themselves and hating themselves for never getting up to face the day. The town was pleasant on the surface: Its lovely bookstores with knowledgeable staff who could talk about authors you couldn't believe you had never heard of; the lived-in restaurants, their booths almost curving to fit the shape of your back; intimate house shows in living rooms and basements with noisy abstract bands that traveled around the country but always insisted on playing in Iowa City, or old, weathered folk artists singing the blues, upholding traditions from a century past. There was a darkness flowing steadily beneath the benevolent chatter and open Midwestern arms. It spoke of dissolute histories—of talking behind one's back, of sleeping with a friend's lover, of taking what was not yours—but even the darkness was appealing: It made the town seem more real, more authentic, and oddly more comfortable. The comfort was treacherous. My arms stuck to the perimeter with gluey satisfaction as if the walls of the city sought to trap me. It was the biggest fear I experienced since moving to Iowa City: The fear of being stuck there, tucked away in a bar booth for the next 10 years, one of those aging, failed writers who didn't make it out to New York, California, or beyond, stuck there with half-finished manuscripts and a few published stories in obscure journals whose copies I kept on my shelf so I could show them to the equally stifled women who came back to my apartment at three in the morning. And in that vision, I was not only a writer, I was not only black, I was not only a failure; I was also the patron saint of inertia, my head forever descended in a puddle of well-distilled rye.

Despite the warning signs, there I was, the Midwestern writer, Iowa's adopted son, sunk-in and comfortable, first a student and eventually just bartending at night, thinking I would rather drink and talk with old friends instead of going home to my desk. And yet, I found myself writing as I had never written before. The city itself was the blueprint for a personal essay, its streets different threads of self-exploration, avenues on the way to complex revelations. The air was vividly alive with ideas, daring challenges against form and radical constructions of voice. You could grab at them as you slid down the street to the bookstore, the coffee shop, or the bar. And the air was dirty too. It was as complex as those who breathed it—echoes of the factory stench blowing south from Cedar Rapids, traces of the farm chem from fields all around us, the dense, inescapable steam in the midst of a heat wave, and the tense, swirling breeze before a spectacular storm.

I took a trip back to San Francisco. The city was undergoing extraordinary change. Waves of development and socio-economic cleansing enveloped its borders, from the coast to the bay. I visited an old friend of mine. We had been bandmates five years earlier. Since then he had vigorously pursued a career in design, studying at exceptional institutions, working internationally, and finally returning to San Francisco to work with a major corporation in Silicon Valley. I toured his apartment in the depths of the Mission District. He and his future wife squeezed their entire lives into an efficient space. He said, "We can't leave this place. You don't understand: this is a great deal." I looked around his cluttered, non-descript dwelling. The relative expanse of our younger years when none of us had much money but somehow lived in large spaces in the center of culture had dwindled to the bare necessities. And these were people with privilege.

Another friend who had grown up in the Bay Area once told me, "It will always be a gold rush town." In its own methodical way, the city instinctively and incessantly chases new visions, pushing out the old. No one can get too comfortable. No one can ever feel safe from change. In the midst of the Great Recession, as the country buckled from a deep housing crisis, real estate values ascended in San Francisco. Tech companies and developers reinvested in neglected neighborhoods, bringing new construction and augmented wealth. When I walked the streets, past the cafés, coffee shops, bars, and increasingly niche-market stores, everything gleamed with an even brighter whiteness than before: bright white citizens looking crisp in their slim-cut trousers, their neat, colorful dresses, smiling as they sipped designer Fair Trade espresso, pushing their bikes and strollers through the Mission and Dolores Park. This was a cosmopolitan breed for which money always came first. They brandished a shining whiteness from which even not all whites were protected. I wondered, if I had stayed, how I would have fit into this new city. On which levels would I have assimilated and in which ways would I have been pushed further from the core? What place was there for a black American in a city where even white people—ones with decent jobs—couldn't maintain their grasp on a dream that had been promised then pulled away? The black population in San Francisco had been 13% in 1970 and by 2010 it was down to 6%. The cleansing had been swift.

The road to the airport cut south toward Silicon Valley. Nestled there in San Mateo County sat the blue-collar haven of South San Francisco, a place to build a middle-class life outside of the incessant hustle of The City. The rents would soon peak there too, edging out some of South City's established residents—many of them of Hispanic heritage. Indeed the struggle stretched in all directions to San Francisco's outlying regions. In Oakland and the towns of the East Bay, the economic challenges of the brown and the poor were cast by formidable opponents who sought to exploit every last square foot for its weight in gold. The gold rush in perpetuity. A fog lifting. The atmosphere of opportunity that had welcomed me to San Francisco many years before had evaporated. If not by desire, the Midwest would become my home by default.

In our first years in Iowa City, Ethan and I had seen each other around town and when we saw each other we nodded, our heads first tilting up, then down, as if to say, "Yo, nigga, what up?" or "I see you, nigga—we in this shit together." We met officially at The Mill. It was a worn-in wooden dive. He was waiting tables and I was drinking beer. We just paused and shook hands.

"You're an actor, right?"

"Yeah, you're a writer?"

"Yeah."

"Cool, I'll see you around, man."

We didn't have to say much. The bond was immediate. It didn't take words because there was something we shared, some intangible experience or weight that we carried around Iowa City from our apartments to the streets, to the workshops, to the bars, and back home every single day. Something that we could feel even if we couldn't touch it. Something that could lie dormant for months, building momentum until it sprung out wildly, falling from the lips of a man who might say, "Damn, those niggers can play."

I was now teaching at the university on a post-graduate fellowship and I had also taken a job bartending and waiting tables at The Mill. Ethan and I hung out after work when the doors closed and the taps loosened. We didn't have an agenda beyond getting drunk and talking about what we were working on; just spending the time together offered some form of relief from the apparition in the air that subtly wore us down. Let's call it isolation. And what might be mistaken solely as the isolation of living in a white college town had really been the 30-year malaise of living in a predominantly white America.

First it was Ethan and I. Then Jeffrey arrived in town. He was young and black and he wanted to be an artist. He enrolled as an undergraduate and signed up for my creative writing class. His essays in workshop revealed his fractured reckoning with what it meant to come of age as a black American citizen. Outside of class, he was often at The Mill, a tall can of Pabst Blue Ribbon in his hand as he talked out the struggles and issues that had confounded his mind. He had grown up in Des Moines and his whole life had been an ongoing confrontation with his father and identity. When he got blackout drunk, which was often, he stood on the patio, wavering unsteadily, not really talking to anyone, and laughing awkwardly at the demons the booze had unearthed. We understood him well and we immediately took him in. It was a process that came naturally: collecting new lonely black artists and giving them a home, even if that home was the slippery allure of beer and whiskey. No one told us that this is what we should do. We just knew it. It was like a script written into our systems, our bloodstreams, our DNA. When the evenings at The Mill ended we retreated to our solitary worlds. Alone we would navigate our individual scenes—the workshop, the theater, the Fox Head. We endured the process and our souls adapted. It had been wired into our minds as a means of surviving the world around us.

I drove to Chicago to attend the panel at the writers' conference to which I had been invited. The city was split in half as if a butcher had put his knife down the middle to separate north from south. We spilled into the Loop where the park opened up to Lake Michigan and where tourists and residents filed happily along Michigan Avenue—the glow of parks, museums, and commerce enticing them to and fro. We entered the hotel conference hall—writers, readers, and publishers, disciples of the literary arts committed to expressions of the human condition yet so removed from the scourge of bullets, poverty, and oppression that marked the city we had come to visit: a split-screen city with realities so incongruent it seemed impossible they had been born of the same mother.

We wore our oxford shirts, corduroy slacks, tweed sports coats, leather hand bags, and Etsy-retail print dresses. We talked of Letters with a capital "L" and discussed movements of the heart as if we and no one else had the most salient grasp on human experience. We talked and drank and aggrandized and felt small and arrogant all at once—we who moved around our protective shell away from the true human suffering that raged unchecked only miles from where we stood. At once I was still a member of the privileged elite *and* the Isolated Negro

Writer of the Midwest, as isolated spiritually, if not physically, as my brothers and sisters and literal cousins who lived on the South Side of Chicago. I drank ales, I drank wines, and they had nothing.

This fractured city, this spectacle of gross American failure. On the surface, Chicago's diversity index was remarkable, but when you peeled the casing you could see that segregation had cornered the majority of the black population into just a quarter of the city's communities. And one third of those black citizens lived beneath the poverty line. My mother believed so deeply in Chicago—the city that had raised her to adulthood. She had gone to college and graduate school there and even still felt that she needed to move beyond the city's glass ceiling on black success. She left her home and in doing so moved from the segregation of her childhood to her adult infiltration of a white world with opportunities not easily afforded to her class, color, or gender. It seemed that in my coming to Iowa and by proxy to Chicago I was not only heading further from East and West Coast foundations but also coming home, returning to my primary roots.

I drank a beer before the panel, adjusted my jacket, straightened my tie, and told them my stories about living in Iowa City: I was black, a writer, living in the Midwest but not from the Midwest, and that Iowa City encouraged a spirited sort of drinking problem. I retreated to my seat alongside the other panelists still jittery from the adrenaline of talking in front of so many people but at peace now that it was done. We cannot group our lives in the way we sometimes strive to group them, into clearly discernible colors: It has the false appearance of making these fraught years easier to understand. A panel concerning what it means to be a Midwestern Writer can never entirely capture what it means to be a Midwestern Writer. There are a million ways to achieve such status. Each of the writers specified their own experiences. They did not posit them as representative of other people who might also look like them: Asian American, queer, white, male, female, and straight. They did not fall into the generalizations of our expected identity performances. We had found a temporary shelter in the reality of messiness rather than the crutch of easy categorization. We shook hands and smiled. The room emptied and we walked away toward our various obligations—readings, discussions, and the hotel bar. As quickly as we had banded together in solidarity, we had found ourselves alone, indistinct. A life more difficult continued its course just beyond our perimeter.

I was at The Mill and it was late. We weren't working, just drinking. We huddled into the nook of the front bar that opened up to the kitchen and the back of the house. Ethan sipped a tumbler of Tullamore D.E.W. The bartender leaned on the back edge of the bar, relaxed. I had a beer in one hand and a tumbler of Maker's sitting in front of me. The television beamed above us but the volume setting had been broken for years. Images flashed and we pieced together narratives without words. The jukebox bellowed out late-night classic rock: Neil Young, Elton John, and Bruce Springsteen. Along the bar, customers gripped their drinks and talked into the final hours of the night. In the seated area, at the four-top tables, young drinkers laughed loudly, the alcohol taking hold.

"Time to get up on outta here, man," Ethan said.

After all the time we had spent in Iowa City, dedicated to our craft, we couldn't see the future. We had exhausted our support from the university. Ethan had decided to leave town. He didn't know where he was going—only that he couldn't stay in Iowa. I understood his drive to break away from the Midwest: a career in acting had a known and difficult route. The final goal—behind a camera in television or film—seemed inescapable to him. His absence would render my time more lonely as a human, as an artist. We didn't spend a lot of time together but knowing that he was there, that he too existed in this confused geography, it made daily life more approachable. I had applied to teaching opportunities in other towns, but they had failed to materialize. I hadn't admitted it aloud but I knew, in my core, that I wouldn't be leaving for some time. I was 31, almost 32, and my future seemed empty.

Donnie walked into the bar. He was tall and he wore loose jeans and a large black jacket though it was warm outside. He had a crisp, rigid big-lid baseball cap on.

"What's up, y'all?" he said, his arms waving and his voice booming.

Ethan just stared into his whiskey. Donnie was a nice guy—always funny and positive. He ordered a drink and wrapped his arms around some friends at the bar. They were right next to us. I said what's up and tipped my beer. A group of college kids on the other side of the room shouted loudly and banged their fists on a table, shaking and clattering the pint glasses. Donnie looked over at them, then back at our huddle at the bar. He shook his head dismissing the young drunks and sarcastically said, "Black people."

He had intended to offer an ironic comment, complaining about the behavior of white people, by using the term "black people" because it would be the unexpected thing to say in the situation while also highlighting that the more common occurrence would have been white people callously complaining about black people. He had braved the murky, stained territory between racism and humor. It might have been funny if Donnie was black, but he was white and that challenged us to consider which side of this gray area we would find ourselves: whether we would side with approval or condemnation. And a further complication: Donnie embraced black stereotypes. His clothes, his vocabulary, and unwavering dedication to rap music seemed to be attributes he had actively acquired from black popular culture rather than the ones that had been passed along by his heritage.

Donnie's condition was not something that had been explained to me, Ethan, or anyone else, but a fact we had come to immediately understand upon first encountering him. At his core he was a good person, who, like us all, sought to shape an identity that suited him. Indeed, what we have collectively been fighting for all along is to be who we want to be, to not have the world's expectations of us nailed to a set of behavioral expectations. Yet, somewhere along his path, Donnie had become too comfortable around the rules of his adopted persona. He had forgotten that in order to inhabit a culture that is not necessarily your own, you must first be sure to not actively offend it. Embrace the culture—yes, embrace any culture that attracts you—but be clear on where you came from. Indulge in jazz, but do not call the jazz players "niggers."

Ethan's calm disposition swelled to anger. He glared at Donnie. "Naw, fuck that. Shit ain't cool, man." He shook his arms at Donnie—not a threat of violence but an imposition on his spiritual comfort. Donnie looked at Ethan, his eyes big, startled. It was the familiar white look: the posture of surprise, astonishment, deep wonder: *How did I get into this situation? I haven't done anything wrong.*

"Dude, what? What's up?" Donnie asked.

"I don't like that shit. Sick of it." Ethan said. I grabbed Ethan. Someone else stepped to Donnie and held him, tried to talk some sense. I pulled Ethan away from the nucleus of tension, out of the main bar and down the hallway toward the back. He cursed and I talked him down and I don't know why I did it. I don't know why I just didn't let him go after Donnie. It was quiet in the back. The main lights had been dimmed and the barstools were on top of the bar.

I took down two stools and poured us beers in small plastic cups. We sat there alongside the bar and sipped our midnight drinks. The moment passed like a wave that had approached intensely, then receded before making its return.

"This shit, man," Ethan said quietly.

His voice sagged with the sad fatigue of defeat. He wanted to get on from Iowa City and I knew it would be soon, but I wondered what he expected to find in his new home. Age had revealed salient truths to us about migration and geography: that perhaps there was no good place to go, that perhaps some places were only less bad than others. The outburst with Donnie hadn't been a watershed moment, it hadn't been a singularly noxious aggression. His words had merely represented another troubling fissure in a plague of divisions. But sometimes even the lightest tremor can loosen the fractured foundations on which we stand. Our lineage is cracked, in dire need of renovation.

We sat on the stools and drank our beers, sinking deeper into the comforting grip of alcohol. The golden glow of the bar lights emanated warmth, a small peace in those dwindling hours.

Heart

Old Models

Dear Emma,

I was down again. I was with my friend Brian who is not really someone I see so much or even care to see so much but when we get together there is a connection. Maybe it's the booze or maybe it's those thick black glasses he wears and that rough, dark haircut that resembles a box. He looks like a 1950s beat and talks with conviction, damns his old film professors for being idiots—the very reason he dropped out of school—and tosses pizzas for a living. He loves noise music and drinks tall glasses of Jim Beam. He's been to jail more than once, gets booked on dumb charges, and ends up sitting there with real criminals. Not to say any of these things are accomplishments in the traditional sense, but really, it's his attitude about it. He pushes through life and understands that there is value in every experience. I am horrified by jail but Brian, who doesn't necessarily like jail, talks about it in a way that isn't spiteful. He sees it as a pit stop he had to make at that time in his life.

We were drunk and I was looking at him, kind of in love with the idea of him. Why do I hang out with people like that, why do I push myself to the other side? What could I possibly be looking for? Why do I need someone like Brian every now and then? Why do I need to get drunk with him, holding on to the edges of the city as we stumble down the road like a bunch of bums? What is it that's missing in me? I suppose we all have an undying interest in the "other," whatever the "other" might be, whether it's dark or light, up or down, right or wrong. I can't quite figure out why I drift so far away from time to time. I think I write these letters to excuse my dark detours, to write off the experiences as research for my words. But there's some deeper reason in me that I have yet to uncover. I think it's the very thing that has kept me from leading a perfect life.

We were wrestling each other—Brian and I—not physically, just pushing ideas on each other as we walked from bar to bar. It was Sunday and the streets in Iowa City were empty, the barfronts quiet. The college kids had retreated into the libraries with books they hadn't read and papers they had only thought about writing. The weekend had left them emptier than they could have possibly imagined. They ordered pizzas and sandwiches but their eyes couldn't focus on the words. They had become murky or absent. We were the real drunks, I suppose. The bars didn't want to be open, and surely some of them were closed, but some of them had to be open because Sunday is the day when we choose not to rest but to continue chasing unfortunate outcomes and evading harsh truths. We left the bars and bought a case of beer and a forty. The forty got tossed in the air and came smashing down to the ground. It probably woke the whole neighborhood and that gave us great pleasure. Somewhere in the midst of this idiocy, I fell on the ground, always falling, and banged my knee. It didn't shatter like the forty: it was just scraped and ugly. We pushed on. In my apartment we were loud and we spilled things. We looked around for inspiration. We burst into my room and looked at my 8-track record player. Yes, it was a record player that also had an 8-track inside of it. It must have been a plaything of the rich when it came out in the 1970s. Now it is merely forgotten, a curious antique in a poor man's room. We plunged one of my few 8-track cassettes into the wide mouth of the player. I had purchased it instead of a plain old record player for these very moments of surprise, bringing a friend home and watching them stare with wonderment at a sunken treasure from a past era. I remember the college student I met in a restaurant one night. We came back to my place and she asked to see my bedroom when I told her about the 8-track. She was so young that the term *8-track* wasn't even an anachronism; for her, it simply didn't exist. This was troubling information for me. I didn't feel bad for her but rather for myself. I should be finding women who are my age. I should be acting my age. I laid her down on the bed and then put a cartridge into the mouth of the 8-track, an old Grateful Dead album, *Skull & Roses*. We kissed on the bed. She didn't care about the nostalgia. As our jeans were coming off, the 8-track ate through the *Skull & Roses* cassette. It hissed viciously and spat out the tape. I could have killed it—that murderer!—it killed my Dead album, it killed me. I'm always going limp just when I think I've made it. She was 19. We passed out.

Brian and I listened to a Patti Smith album called *Radio Ethiopia* on the 8-track. We were sitting there listening to Patti and all I could think of was that infamous jab Lou Reed had once lobbed at Smith on his live *Take No Prisoners* album: "Fuck Radio Ethiopia / This is Radio Brooklyn." That was in 1978, Reed on his last legs of decadence, a drunk, a speed-freak, an aging punk. A few years later he would re-emerge sober with a wife. In the mid '70s he had dated a trans woman. He had effectively discontinued an old model of himself, preferring literary elder statesman to burned-out proto-punk. Brian and I talked of Lou Reed for a bit and then we covered ourselves in blankets to keep out the cold.

When I awoke it was hell and the sun was out. I discovered I had lost several important items from the night before: a book I hadn't finished reading, a purse, and an iPod I had purchased on eBay. There was a smell in the apartment of wet cats though we were the only animals. The air sagged with the sweaty film of dirty men who have thrown up their last hopes in an effort to reclaim the fractured pieces of dissipated youth.

We went to The Mill to eat cheeseburgers and Brian read my copy of James Baldwin's *Notes of a Native Son* over his lunch. He homed in on a particular essay, "Equal in Paris," about Baldwin's experience of going to jail in France. Brian talked about his own jail experience in Iowa City. I asked him, "Who else was in jail, a bunch of fraternity drunks?" He just looked at me, as plainly as he could and said, "No man, it was just black people," and that was the saddest thing I had ever heard: deep in the core of a white college town and all of the people in jail were still a bunch of worn-down black people. There was no hope for us anywhere. This country and its systems suffocated us at every turn. He said they called him "Glasses" in jail because of his thick-framed spectacles. They made fun of him but never roughed him up. He saw a couple of guys beat the crap out of each other and he said the food was terrible. He had been to jail in Cedar Rapids too and he said that was a real place to get your ass kicked but the food had been much better, almost good.

I came home. My knee hurt and I looked at the wound. I could see then that it was really torn up. It was bright, a loud reddish color like a stop sign. My apartment was soaked in beer and trash. I hated myself for being so drunk and broken up. I wanted to get that feeling out of me as soon as I could but I had been there before and I knew it would take at least a week to feel normal again. And that's the problem with Sunday nights and drinking: it throws the whole week into disarray, makes it impossible to reset or start over. I wish the bar hadn't been selling good whiskey for three dollars or smiling at me as I slid further from coherence or self-respect. What were they thinking: don't they know I have a problem?

Just then, half-asleep on my couch with my insides hurting all over, I thought of you and I knew that I liked you and that you might be some sort of light I could follow on my way out of the cave. I went to the 8-track in my room and put on Patti Smith. I didn't like the album much, but given my fragile, beat-up, fake-artist's state of mind, it was the only thing I could do.

Yours,

A.

Interstate

Dear Emma,

I was going 80 miles per hour down the interstate. The freezing rain was coming down fluidly and forming crystalline glaciers on my windshield. I had been on the road for about nine hours and I was making incredible time. I was going to get there so early. I was going to set a new record. I pulled into the left lane. I had the audacity to pass a truck. He was going about 70 and that was way too slow. I was far enough ahead of him that I decided to pull back over into the right lane. I had to bend down over the steering wheel—it was so hard to see anything out of the window with all of that ice clutching at my windshield. Suddenly the car turned inward to the left and then swished around to the right. It only took a second and a half.

Oddly calm, I acknowledged that I was no longer driving, no longer controlling the situation—the car and I, we were floating above the road on a smooth layer of ice. The truck was coming up behind me, going 70. I didn't try to turn back. I just pressed down steadily on the brakes and let the car take its course. I wasn't sure where we were going but I tried to slow us down, to alleviate the pain of the impact. It didn't seem like we were going so fast anymore.

There was a stark beauty to it, sliding around America at night in a sturdy metal box. For a moment the car wasn't a car but a small room I was sitting in, careening back and forth as in a strong Californian earthquake. I saw that we had finally settled on a course heading directly at the right snowbank. Everything in the car began to shift and I thought, almost at peace, "Well, this is it." We soared off the road and into the ditch.

The car had firmly planted itself in a plot of icy grass. I was alive. Bob Dylan's "Love Minus Zero/No Limit" was playing on the stereo: *the bridge at midnight trembles*... It seemed absurd, though any song at that moment would have seemed absurd. The truck zipped by on the interstate. What was that driver thinking about me and my hubris? I got out of the car and looked around to assess any damage. It was cold and I was slipping all over the grass. My car looked okay. I got back in the driver's seat.

I tried driving directly out of the ditch but that was impossible. Instead I put the car in first and backed up a bit so that I was in the flat part of the ditch. From there I drove slightly up the hill in increments so that I could make it back to the shoulder and onto the road. I gathered myself and slowly pushed onto the highway, first going 40 then 50. I noticed then that, in the midst of the ice storm, most cars were going that speed. Eventually I turned the stereo back on but I took that Dylan album off. It horrified me now. I listened to Marble Sky; ambient and glacial waves of sound undulated throughout the car. I worked my way up the road, feeling like less of a man or a role model yet older and wiser. I had spoken to my parents on the phone earlier from the road and they had said, *Be careful*. And though I had known then that they were right I only now truly understood them. As I drove I wondered if every piece of wisdom they had shared with me had been matched by some similar experience. It was then that I knew to some degree what it meant to be a parent and to live a long, full life. I thought of you and the future children we might have. I moved slowly but with confidence into the night.

Yours,

A.

Americana/Dying of Thirst

Dear Emma,

I was in Iowa City in the student union for a concert and I was surrounded by over 1800 white people. I was alone. I was the smallest black man in the world. Outside, the air was warm and dry. Summer had yet to touch down with its fever-heat and thick humidity. Inside, the bodies steamed up the room. Everyone looked so young. I stood near the back where the congestion thinned out. Up front, it was wild, the students fervent in their adoration, their devotion to the man on stage: Kendrick Lamar. He had rolled onto the platform dressed in a black crewneck sweatshirt, charcoal jeans, and white high-tops. He wore a Yankees hat, the "NY" logo surrounded by two hashtags like this: #NY#. He looked down at us from the stage and asked, "What the fuck am I doing in Iowa?"

The students erupted. Their rolling arms, bent legs, and hunched bodies all resembled so well the clips they had seen on YouTube. Most everyone knew the lyrics to the songs and many people sang them aloud. At certain moments, the interplay between artist and audience elevated to a call and response. Kendrick bounced around the stage, singing and shouting his songs, smiling at the floor of students in front of him. When a song finished, the kids stood up tall with their hands in the air, looking like corn crop in late summer, ready for picking, ready for consumption.

I was enthralled, less with Kendrick and more with the scene. I marveled at how the deeply considered music of a black man from Los Angeles could resonate so vigorously with a white student body from Chicagoland and Iowa. I wanted to understand how much of what he meant by his words had possibly been lost or actively discarded in translation. I wanted to understand why an album—Kendrick's *good kid, m.A.A.d city*—that I felt so connected to on headphones now seemed like it was several acres away, with the divide of college students between me and the artist on stage. I was getting queasy—my hands were sweating and my face turned hot—and I didn't quite understand why. I inched back slowly with each song, getting closer to the venue's exit.

The beat from "m.A.A.d city" dropped in like a series of disorienting thunder-claps. It was shocking, it was amazing. Something detonated in the students around me—they left their feet, their eyes glossed over with fascination. The opening hook unfolded and I sensed immediately there would be a problem. As Kendrick sang, "Man down, where you from, nigga?" and the ensuing lines all ending with a declaration of the n-word, it seemed as if the entire room chimed in, shouting along with genuine enthusiasm. The roar of almost 2,000 white people shouting "nigga" in a room with a black man on stage took on an odd quality, like a twisted reshaping of a rally of nationalists and fascists. I looked around me, peering at the enthusiastic youth and felt almost entirely alone, separated from my music, my blues, my town, my identity. Kendrick beamed on stage, energized by the power, the taut grip of his music.

I backed out of the concert hall more intently than before. I walked outside where it was warm, quiet, and entirely serene. I wondered: is this the legacy rap has left us with? Do these students understand the blues that run so deeply in Kendrick's songs? Do they understand that these are work-songs, god-songs, gospels, redemptions as much as they are anthems for parties with kegs and cocaine and university-branded sweat-shirts? In the far-away future, when they—the people who have survived humanity's current savagery—look back at our culture and study our music what will they call rap? Will they call it by that name or will one hundred years from blues to jazz to rap come to be understood as one insistent call from a tired but endlessly resilient and expressive people? Will they simply call it: Americana? Will they understand that the more pain we faced the more creative we became, that our music of emotional slavery was not just a series of notes and figures and rhythms? That when we said "slavery" we didn't just mean ours, we meant yours too. That when we wrote songs, they were more than songs, they were the texts of American history itself.

Kendrick, Lady Day, Howlin' Wolf. These songs are civil wars, are emancipations, are movements for deferred liberties, are the sorrows of systematic isolation, and are the joys of understanding that a fractured life is still life nonetheless. And fractured lives are not just black lives but Native lives, immigrant lives, and white lives too—the whole continent. So when we sing this Americana songbook we should be awake and know that when we sing someone else's song we are also singing our own.

My head was full of confusion as it often is. I briefly considered seeking solace in the bar, in glasses of whiskey and beer—always my easiest escape. But my compass endured and I climbed the hill toward my home, toward you. I knew I would find warmth by your side—it is the place I go when I have been left alone or have stumbled by my own stupid actions.

I fall into your arms as I always do, as I always will. Your skin is as pale as mine is dark. And in that way, we are America too.

Love,

A.

Acknowledgments

Deepest gratitude to my parents, my brother, sister-in-law, nieces and nephews, my dearest wife and daughter, my extended family, and excellent in-laws.

Thank you to the teachers and advisors who shared so much: Donna Denize, Malcolm Lester, P. Adams Sitney, Su Friedrich, Aleta Hayes, Pamela Holm, David Hamilton, Bonnie Sunstein, Vershawn Ashanti Young, Susan Lohafer, Mary Ruefle, Patricia Foster, Robin Hemley, John D'Agata, and Ken Foster.

Thank you to the team at Two Dollar Radio that believed in this work: Eric & Eliza Obenauf, and Molly Delaney.

Thank you to the editors who shaped early versions of this material: Barrie Jean Borich, Jodee Stanley, Zachary Burkhart, and Yuka Igarishi. A special thank you to Steve Woodward and Caroline Casey for their time and guidance on the earliest draft of this manuscript.

Much love to all of my best friends and coworkers for your support and fellowship—as well as to my current, former, and future bandmates, in particular to John Lindenbaum who has driven all over America with me a thousand times to find out who we are.

To all of the artists and thinkers across and between mediums: thank you for the work and brilliance you are putting into this world.

Two Dollar Radio
Books too loud to Ignore

ALSO AVAILABLE Here are some other titles you might want to dig into.

SAVAGE GODS BY PAUL KINGSNORTH

← "Kingsnorth's is a voice worth listening to." —*Kirkus Reviews*

"For all the confessional memoirs so popular at the moment, this is the real deal." —*The American Conservative*

SAVAGE GODS ASKS, can words ever paint the truth of the world—or are they part of the great lie which is killing it?

THE BOOK OF X NOVEL BY SARAH ROSE ETTER

← "Etter brilliantly, viciously lays bare what it means to be a woman in the world, what it means to hurt, to need, to want, so much it consumes everything." —Roxane Gay

"A powerful novel." —*Minneapolis Star-Tribune*

A SURREAL EXPLORATION OF ONE WOMAN'S LIFE and death against a landscape of meat, office desks, and bad men.

TRIANGULUM NOVEL BY MASANDE NTSHANGA

← "Magnificently disorienting and meticulously constructed, *Triangulum* couples an urgent subtext with an unceasing sense of mystery. This is a thought-provoking dream of a novel, situated within thought-provoking contexts both fictional and historical." —Tobias Carroll, Tor.com

AN AMBITIOUS, OFTEN PHILOSOPHICAL AND GENRE-BENDING NOVEL that covers a period of over 40 years in South Africa's recent past and near future.

THE WORD FOR WOMAN IS WILDERNESS
NOVEL BY ABI ANDREWS

← "Unlike any published work I have read, in ways that are beguiling, audacious…" —Sarah Moss, *The Guardian*

THIS IS A NEW KIND OF NATURE WRITING — one that crosses fiction with science writing and puts gender politics at the center of the landscape.

AWAY! AWAY! NOVEL BY JANA BEŇOVÁ
TRANSLATED BY JANET LIVINGSTONE

→ **Winner of the European Union Prize for Literature**

← "Beňová's short, fast novels are a revolution against normality." —Austrian Broadcasting Corporation, ORF

WITH MAGNETIC, SPARKLING PROSE, Beňová delivers a lively mosaic that ruminates on human relationships, our greatest fears and desires.

Books to read!

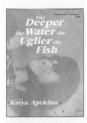

THE DEEPER THE WATER THE UGLIER THE FISH NOVEL BY **KATYA APEKINA**

→ **2018** *Los Angeles Times* **Book Prize Finalist**

← "Brilliantly structured... refreshingly original, and the writing is nothing short of gorgeous. It's a stunningly accomplished book." —Michael Schaub, NPR

POWERFULLY CAPTURES THE QUIET TORMENT of two sisters craving the attention of a parent they can't, and shouldn't, have to themselves.

THE BLURRY YEARS NOVEL BY **ELEANOR KRISEMAN**

← "Kriseman's is a new voice to celebrate."
—*Publishers Weekly*

THE BLURRY YEARS IS A POWERFUL and unorthodox coming-of-age story from an assured new literary voice, featuring a stirringly twisted mother-daughter relationship, set against the sleazy, vividly-drawn backdrop of late-seventies and early-eighties Florida.

THE UNDERNEATH NOVEL BY **MELANIE FINN**

← "*The Underneath* is an excellent thriller." —*Star Tribune*

THE UNDERNEATH IS AN INTELLIGENT and considerate exploration of violence—both personal and social—and whether violence may ever be justified. With the assurance and grace of her acclaimed novel *The Gloaming*, Melanie Finn returns with a precisely layered and tense new literary thriller.

PALACES NOVEL BY **SIMON JACOBS**

← "*Palaces* is robust, both current and clairvoyant... With a pitch-perfect portrayal of the punk scene and idiosyncratic, meaty characters, this is a wonderful novel that takes no prisoners." —*Foreword Reviews*, starred review

WITH INCISIVE PRECISION and a cool detachment, Simon Jacobs has crafted a surreal and spellbinding first novel of horror and intrigue.

THEY CAN'T KILL US UNTIL THEY KILL US ESSAYS BY **HANIF ABDURRAQIB**

→ **Best Books 2017:** NPR, *Buzzfeed, Paste Magazine, Esquire, Chicago Tribune, Vol. 1 Brooklyn,* CBC (Canada), *Stereogum, National Post* (Canada), *Entropy, Heavy, Book Riot, Chicago Review of Books* (November), *The Los Angeles Review, Michigan Daily*

← "Funny, painful, precise, desperate, and loving throughout. Not a day has sounded the same since I read him."
—Greil Marcus, *Village Voice*

Books to read!

WHITE DIALOGUES STORIES BENNETT SIMS

← "Anyone who admires such pyrotechnics of language will find 21st-century echoes of Edgar Allan Poe in Sims' portraits of paranoia and delusion."
—*New York Times Book Review*

IN THESE ELEVEN STORIES, Sims moves from slow-burn psychological horror to playful comedy, bringing us into the minds of people who are haunted by their environments, obsessions, and doubts.

FOUND AUDIO NOVEL BY N.J. CAMPBELL

← "[A] mysterious work of metafiction... dizzying, arresting and defiantly bold." —*Chicago Tribune*

← "This strange little book, full of momentum, intrigue, and weighty ideas to mull over, is a bona fide literary page-turner." —*Publishers Weekly*, "Best Summer Books, 2017"

SEEING PEOPLE OFF NOVEL BY JANA BEŇOVÁ
TRANSLATED BY JANET LIVINGSTONE

⇢ **Winner of the European Union Prize for Literature**

← "A fascinating novel. Fans of inward-looking post-modernists like Clarice Lispector will find much to admire."
—NPR

A KALEIDOSCOPIC, POETIC, AND DARKLY FUNNY portrait of a young couple navigating post-socialist Slovakia.

THE DROP EDGE OF YONDER
NOVEL BY RUDOLPH WURLITZER

← "One of the most interesting voices in American fiction."
—*Rolling Stone*

AN EPIC ADVENTURE that explores the truth and temptations of the American myth, revealing one of America's most transcendant writers at the top of his form.

THE VINE THAT ATE THE SOUTH
NOVEL BY J.D. WILKES

← "Undeniably one of the smartest, most original Southern Gothic novels to come along in years." — Michael Schaub, NPR

WITH THE ENERGY AND UNIQUE VISION that established him as a celebrated musician, Wilkes here is an accomplished storyteller on a Homeric voyage that strikes at the heart of American mythology.

Books to read!

NOT DARK YET NOVEL BY **BERIT ELLINGSEN**

← "Fascinating, surreal, gorgeously written."
—*BuzzFeed*

ON THE VERGE OF a self-inflicted apocalypse, a former military sniper is enlisted by a former lover for an eco-terrorist action that threatens the quiet life he built for himself in the mountains.

THE GLACIER NOVEL BY **JEFF WOOD**

← "Gorgeously and urgently written."
—*Library Journal*, starred review

FOLLOWING A CATERER AT a convention center, a surveyor residing in a storage unit, and the masses lining up for an Event on the horizon, *The Glacier* is a poetic rendering of the pre-apocalypse.

HAINTS STAY NOVEL BY **COLIN WINNETTE**

← "In his astonishing portrait of American violence, Colin Winnette makes use of the Western genre to stunning effect." —*Los Angeles Times*

HAINTS STAY IS A NEW Acid Western in the tradition of Rudolph Wurlitzer, *Meek's Cutoff*, and Jim Jarmusch's *Dead Man*: meaning it is brutal, surreal, and possesses an unsettling humor.

THE ONLY ONES NOVEL BY **CAROLA DIBBELL**

→ **Best Books 2015:** *Washington Post*; *O, The Oprah Magazine*; NPR
← "Breathtaking." —NPR

INEZ WANDERS A POST-PANDEMIC world immune to disease. Her life is altered when a grief-stricken mother that hired her to provide genetic material backs out, leaving Inez with the product: a baby girl.

BINARY STAR NOVEL BY **SARAH GERARD**

→ *Los Angeles Times* Book Prize Finalist
→ **Best Books 2015:** *BuzzFeed*, *Vanity Fair*, NPR
← "Rhythmic, hallucinatory, yet vivid as crystal." —NPR

AN ELEGIAC, INTENSE PORTRAIT of two young lovers as they battle their personal afflictions while on a road trip across the U.S.